Real life, real answers.

Financial planning for the two-career family

Real life, real answers.

Financial planning for the two-career family

by
Candace E. Trunzo

Houghton Mifflin Company   Boston

1990

For information about permission to reproduce selections from this book, write to Permissions, Houghton Mifflin Company, 2 Park Street, Boston, Massachusetts 02108.

Library of Congress Catalog Card Number: 89-85919
ISBN: 0-395-51097-X

General editors: Barbara Binswanger, James Charlton, Lee Simmons

Design by Hudson Studio

"Real life, real answers" is a trademark of the John Hancock Mutual Life Insurance Company.

Printed in the United States of America

10 9 8 7 6 5 4 3 2 1

Although this book is designed to provide accurate and authoritative information in regard to the subject matter covered, neither the author and general editors nor the publisher are engaged in rendering legal, accounting, or other professional service. If legal advice or other expert assistance is required, the services of a competent professional should be sought.

Contents

CHAPTER I

Coping with two careers

Most contemporary two-career couples come from one-career families. Our parents married, bought a house, had children right away, and lived their lives à la *Leave It to Beaver*. Dad was off to work each morning and mom stayed at home (we didn't call what she did "work" back then). But we, their kids, better known as the baby boom generation, have been following a brand-new script ever since. Today there are 26.7 million two-paycheck couples; 17.8 million of those have children living at home.

We are twice as likely as our parents to have gone to college. We have helped change the mores of our society, liberating women from their traditional roles and choosing to live together in lieu of or before marriage. When we do marry, it is hardly in haste. Then we put off having children in order to pursue demanding careers and other pleasures. We want to do it all and in our own sweet time. But we have had few role models to guide us.

Whether you are a two-income couple without kids or a working couple whose tribe has increased, combining busy careers, family life, and finances is quite a juggling act. Certainly, our financial lives are complicated enough: in the space of a decade we have had to deal with the repercussions of bank deregulation, a myriad of new financial products and services, tax reform, a recession, inflation, a real estate boom, and a stock market crash. While two incomes can give couples a financial edge (44 percent of two-career families have an income

1

of $40,000 or more), that edge is often blunted by poor planning. Not only financial stability but family stability can suffer if there is no management or compromise in a two-career family.

Couples without children—and there are about 4 million married couples who are child-free—clearly have a different agenda and a different set of challenges than their counterparts with kids. Dubbed DINKS (dual income, no kids), this demographic subset can often afford to aim for goals such as early retirement or entrepreneurship—goals that are only pipe dreams to other families. Sarah and Paul Mariano of Santa Fe, for example, are a professional couple who have been married for seven years. Kids are not part of the master plan of this 30-something couple, but quitting work in their early fifties and traveling around the world are.

The main obstacle for the Marianos and couples like them: impulse spending. Learning how to cut back on the good life is essential if they are going to meet their goals. With a minimum of fixed costs to be concerned with, DINKS should be able to save up to 20 percent of their gross income for an early and comfortable retirement. Another concern for couples without children is taxes. Without careful tax planning, DINKS can lose a substantial chunk of their earnings to taxes.

Life gets even more complicated when you add children to the two-career equation. The rewards of a challenging career and a loving child are great. Yet coping with both at the same time can put a strain on the best of marriages. Not every mom is super, not every dad lives up to his liberated label, and not every nanny—for those families who can afford to hire one—comes with Mary Poppins's bag of tricks. The only way to cope is to compromise. He wakes early for the 6 a.m. feeding so she won't be late for her 8 a.m. meeting. She skips a Saturday morning yoga class so he can get in 18 holes of golf. And both bid farewell to those lazy, quiet Sundays together over brunch and the newspapers.

These couples, too, have to learn how to control the unbridled spending habits left over from their childless days. They have to start putting money away for their children's college education, their own retirement, and other important goals and responsibilities. They have to make sure that their families are protected should something happen to them. And while they do all that, they must manage the household, get that promotion, and be mommy or daddy of the century.

Having two incomes and two careers in one family gives you a different set of financial problems and opportunities than your parents had. This book looks at all the elements of personal finance from the perspective of a two-career couple. Whether you have children or not, you will find some of the strategies outlined in the pages that follow useful in getting your two-income financial house in order.

CHAPTER II

Where does all the money go?

Never have so many earned so much and saved so little. Taxes certainly account for a big chunk of your paycheck. Inflation is another culprit. Some couples are still struggling to pay off student loans; others have saved almost exclusively through home ownership and find themselves house poor, with little spare cash after paying the mortgage and other bills.

Yet for a considerable number of two-career couples, the reason for their inability to save is simply the urge to splurge. Especially if you have no children, why pass up those romantic weekend jaunts to the Florida Keys, those ultimate driving machines or evenings at the ballet? You're homebodies? Well, the accoutrements of couch potatoes are particularly pricey: whirlpool baths, video cassette recorders, CD players, home computers, not to mention the cushiest of couches. But even if you favor Big Macs, vacation at Lake Lowkey, and drive a Yugo, you're probably spending more and monitoring what you spend less than single-earner families.

In order to start saving or increase your savings you must get control of your cash flow. To do that, you must figure out your current spending habits. You may be shocked at what you find. Laurie and Mark Gross of Manhattan, with a combined income of almost $100,000, were stunned when a financial planner who was helping them with budgeting pointed out that they were spending $14,000 a year on restaurant meals. The couple was quickly put on a financial diet and they are now saving regularly. To determine just where you're most vulnerable, you'll need to come up with a cash-flow statement that summarizes your earnings and expenses for the past year. Use the worksheet on page 9.

First add up your income. Your most recent tax return is probably your best source for toting up your salaries, interest, dividends, bonuses, or commissions. You will have to adjust those figures if you have recently received a $20,000 inheritance or some other windfall. Then move to the expense side of your balance sheet. Take your total tax bill from your return as well, making sure you include what was due as well as withheld. Your Social Security tax will be on your copy of the W-2 form.

Then start calculating your fixed expenses, things like your mortgage or rent, property taxes, car payments, and insurance premium expenses. Other fixed and predictable expenses could range from a nanny's weekly salary to bimonthly haircuts.

Now you must account for that never-never land of ever-changing expenses that could give even Peter Pan gray hairs: clothes, books and magazines, presents, bottles of Bordeaux, food, and laundry and dry cleaning. The best way to track this haphazard spending is by going through a year's worth of checks. A year's worth is necessary to make sure you pick up all once-a-year expenses and seasonal influences on spending such as Christmas or summer vacations. Divide the checks into corresponding categories, such as dining out, clothing, and food, on your cash-flow statement.

Checks made out to American Express, Visa, and other credit card companies or department stores will be impossible to categorize. You will have to hunt up corresponding statements for each account and tally each charge in the appropriate category. As you look over these statements, it may be worthwhile to note how large your outstanding balances are and how much you have incurred in non-tax-deductible finance charges over the 12-month period. Enough to buy a beach bar on St. Thomas and retire, you say? Then you had better make less use of your cards and pay more promptly as you assess ways to build up your surplus.

In your attempt to track where all the money goes, you will undoubtedly be thwarted by those black holes of family budgets: checks made out to cash and automatic teller machine (ATM) withdrawal slips. Perhaps you could keep a diary of cash expenditures for at least one month. If more than 30 percent of your after-tax income consists of cash expenditures, you will have to rethink the way you keep tabs on your money. If you are not disciplined enough to steer clear of those ATMs, consider not carrying your card around with you; retrieve it only in an emergency.

THE BOTTOM LINE

After you have figured out how you spent your two incomes, deduct your total outgo from your income. What is left—if anything—is what you could or should have for savings and investments. If you have a negative number at the bottom of your balance sheet, then you probably borrowed or took some money from savings or investments to make ends meet. If debt seems to be a chronic problem—and it is for many two-career couples—you may need some credit counseling (see Chapter III).

Now that you have a handle on how you spend, you can take the necessary action to fritter away less and save up more toward your goals: buying a car, starting a family, investing for retirement. The first thing you must do is to look over your categories of expenditures to see where you can do some pruning. That doesn't mean that you have to eliminate all the things that bring you pleasure. Rather, consume less conspicuously in smaller, easier-to-swallow ways. Assuming you spend an average of $10 a day to eat lunch, bringing your lunch to work instead of eating out could save you more than $2,000 a year—and an untold number of calories in the bargain. Raising the deductibles on your insurance premiums, cutting down on your weekend getaways, and shopping at outlets rather than "in" boutiques are other options to consider. Even if you have surplus funds, you should take a close look at your spending patterns to make sure you are satisfied with how you spend those two incomes. Perhaps you have been saving but would like to save even more. Most two-income families can save at least 10 percent of their after-tax income without too much strain.

SAVING SYSTEMATICALLY

With some adjustments, you should be able to come up with a budget that will provide you with the excess cash to fund your goals. The issue is how you can guarantee that this operating surplus will go into savings and investments rather than be frittered away. The key to success is making your savings an integral part of your budget instead of regarding savings as anything left over after you've spent in the manner to which you have become accustomed. Just as you pay your mortgage and your telephone bill each month, you pay your savings or investment plan. If you are not disciplined enough to do this yourself, then put the money into a payroll savings plan. You can't spend what you can't get your hands on. You could also arrange with your bank to automatically transfer a specific amount from your checking account each month into an interest–bearing savings or investment account.

LOVE AND MONEY

Of course, it's one thing to tell a couple to cut back in a few areas or determine what their financial goals should be; it's quite another to get them to agree on those cutbacks or how to achieve those goals. People have different emotional responses toward money—to some money represents love, to others status, and to still others security. Tensions can mount between people who have been brought up differently and have different responses toward money. Indeed, having different attitudes toward how money is saved or spent can be even more of a problem for a two-career couple than not having enough money. If one of you comes from a long line of penny-pinchers and the other is the last of the big spenders, you are going to have a lot of negotiating to do. On the other hand, husbands and wives with similar economic backgrounds are more likely to share the same attitudes toward money and have less trouble in their financial lives.

Communication and compromise along with some solid planning are the ways to deal with disputes about money. If you do not know who spends how much for what, the chances are great that you will have something to quibble about. But by working out a budget together that takes both of your needs and concerns into consideration, you can avoid most conflicts. If you agree that each of you is entitled to some "mad money," decide how much and perhaps set up different checking accounts for those kinds of purchases. You might also want to set an upper limit on how much each of you can spend on a purchase without consulting the other partner. If you have disparate incomes and do not pool your money, you might want to contribute to various funds by using percentages rather than flat dollar amounts. If one of you earns $75,000 and the other $25,000, for example, it might be more equitable for each of you to put 5 percent of your earnings toward buying a vacation home rather than kick in $2,500 each.

To mingle or not to mingle—for most couples it is a question of sentiment. For others, it is one of practicality. If you often charge business expenses on your personal card or frequently

HOW GOES YOUR CASH FLOW?

To determine how you are spending your money—and how much you should have left over for savings—fill in this cash-flow statement for the past 12-month period.

What comes in

His salary _____

Her salary _____

Dividends and/or interest income _____

Child support or alimony _____

Other _____

Total _____

What goes out

Income tax _____

Social Security tax _____

Property tax _____

Rent or mortgage payments (including homeowners insurance) _____

Dining in (groceries, etc.) _____

Dining out _____

Clothing _____

Child care _____

Telephone _____

Utilities _____

Furniture and other objects for the home _____

Vacations and recreation _____

Car expenses (payments, repairs, gas, insurance) _____

Medical insurance _____

Life and disability insurance _____

Household repairs and maintenance _____

Credit card interest _____

Loan payments _____

Gifts _____

Haircuts, manicures, etc. _____

Other _____

Total _____

Surplus (what comes in minus what goes out) _____

THE COST OF CHILDREN TO AGE 18

According to studies done by Thomas J. Espenshade and Charles A. Calhoun at the Urban Institute in Washington, D.C., children make a bigger dent in the family budget than one might think. Besides direct expenses—food, clothing, shelter, and so on—the chart includes "opportunity" costs, such as income mothers forgo by staying at home to care for their children. College costs are not included.

| | Socioeconomic status (a) | | |
	Low	Middle	High
Direct expenditures (b)	$ 78,500	$ 85,100	$ 101,500
Opportunity costs (b)(c)	22,000	24,000	25,500
Total	$ 100,500	$ 109,100	$ 127,000

(a) Reflects family income and husband's education and occupation in white families. "Low" SES means average family income of $22,000 per year, less than a high school education, and a blue-collar job; "middle" means average family income of $28,000 per year, a high school education, and a blue-collar job; "high" means average family income of $42,000 per year, education beyond high school, and a white-collar job.
(b) In 1981 prices.
(c) Estimated by multiplying hours lost from paid employment by hourly wage rate.

---

write business-related checks, it is tidier to have separate accounts. If you are part of a stepfamily you may need both joint and separate accounts (see Chapter IX). On the other hand, many couples find it easier to pool their resources and their assets, and sometimes it makes sense to do so.

WHEN BABY MAKES THREE

When children enter the picture, it is time to mix a new fiscal formula. Indeed, the money matters you could afford to overlook as DINKS take on compelling significance when you assume the responsibility of parenthood. The first year of a child's life is particularly pricey. Insurance will probably cover about two-thirds of the cost of routine hospital and delivery expenses, which run about $2,500, depending on where you live. But routine checkups—those monthly visits to the pediatrician's office during the first year—are usually not reimbursable and cost $400 or more. The number of sick visits, especially when it comes to your firstborn, can almost double that figure.

Then consider those necessities of babyhood: clothing, diapers, crib, changing table, car seat, playpen, high chair, toys, and more toys (a pitfall for many guilt-ridden two-career couples). Factor in increased food costs, too—about 20 percent more from day one if the mother is not nursing, from month six if she is. Not only will you have a new mouth to feed, but with your time at a premium, you and your spouse will probably wind up eating more than your share of expensive frozen conve-nience foods and take-out meals. Depending on the type of child care you choose (see Chapter IV), you will have to budget anywhere from $400 to $1,200 a month.

JUST IN CASE

Once you have your spending habits under control, you will be able to start thinking about putting some money away for the really expensive part of child rearing: college. Before you tie up any money in investments, however, you ought to have at least three months' living expenses—now that you know what they are—put aside in an emergency fund. Children make it even more likely that expenses, particularly medical ones, will pop up unexpectedly. You should also have that extra cushion in case either mom or dad uses up any paid leave and opts to spend another few months with the baby. Also, if one member of a two-career family loses a job, this reserve can make the difference between settling for a less than satisfactory position or waiting for the right opportunity.

Since this money should be readily available, the best places to park it are in money market mutual funds and ac-counts, short-term certificates of deposit, or Treasury bills. If you find it impossible to come up with enough emergency cash

Real life, real answers.

When Anna and Sam Rudd were married two years ago, they agreed to pool their joint income of $65,000. Since Anna, an architect, felt insecure about paying the bills and balancing the books, Sam, a business school professor, took on the job. For a while, the newlyweds lived in balanced bliss. But in the second year of their marriage, Sam began to feel not only put upon by the bookkeeping burden but bewildered by checks that Anna would take from the checkbook and forget to enter, cash withdrawals from the automatic teller machines that he had no knowledge of, and bottom lines that wouldn't match. When Anna bought a $200 leather briefcase without consulting Sam, he blew his stack. The couple was hoping to save an undetermined amount for a down payment on a home of their own in the next 5 years, but at the rate they were saving, it would take 15 years.

The problem was that the Rudds had never made a budget for themselves; they never set limits on certain types of spending and never set specific goals on what they would save. After a family pow-wow, the couple worked out their financial differences. They agreed that they would take turns paying bills and balancing the books each month. They also determined that they would need to save $35,000 for their dream house. Anna vowed that she would limit her spending to help them achieve their goal. They also decided that they would not make any purchase of more than $100 without consulting one another.

to stash away, and you have no big debt problems, you could use a home equity line of credit or an unsecured credit line (see Chapter IV) to tide you over in an emergency. Funding an emergency account should be a first priority before you begin any other savings or investment plan.

CHAPTER III

Making the most of what you've got

B esides investing, there are two ways for couples to make the most of what they've got: minimize their debt and maximize their tax savings. Never has it been more difficult to do either, thanks to easier credit and tougher tax laws.

THE QUESTION OF CREDIT

Many two-career couples are in over their heads. It is no wonder, for this is the age of easy credit. Home-equity loans are promoted like "oldie but goody" record collections on late-night television. Unsolicited credit cards—or at least preapproved applications—arrive with the frequency of junk mail. Factor in mortgage costs and the decline in real household income over the past decade and it is hardly surprising that credit counseling services, which count many well-heeled two-earner families among their clientele, say business is booming.

A decade or so ago borrowing made economic sense. No longer. There are three solid reasons to think twice about borrowing today. First, we are no longer in the inflationary spiral of the 1970's. Buying now and paying later was smart when anything you bought one year cost much more the next. Who cared if you didn't really need that automatic sushi slicer or the even smaller, sleeker Walkman than the two you already had? But with inflation in the low single digits, borrowing is no longer a bonanza.

The tax reform law has also made borrowing less appealing. Before the 1986 tax law passed you could deduct all your interest payments. While you can still write off the interest on the mortgage for your primary residence or your vacation home (as well as interest on home equity loans, explained below), the interest deduction on consumer loans will be phased out for good in 1991 (it is a measly 10 percent in 1990). Lower income tax rates make any interest deductions left less worthwhile.

Then there's the question of the high cost of borrowing. In mid-1989 interest rates for most consumer loans were 18 to 20 percent. If you took $2,000 and used it to pay off your credit card balances, you could save 18 percent a year—$360—before taxes. That's almost three times as much as you would earn by putting the same amount in a money market fund.

How much can you handle?

Keep all nonmortgage debt to an absolute minimum. But if you are going to borrow, credit advisers say that you should keep your consumer debt payments down to 10 to 15 percent of your total monthly net income—that is, your total income less all income tax, Social Security tax, and pension contributions. If you are a working couple taking home at least $50,000, you can probably carry 15 percent. But if you have children, make it less than 10 percent. This includes payments due on credit cards and personal, school, and car loans, but not first mortgages, home equity loans, or rent. Add those costs, and you should be spending a maximum of 33 to 36 percent of your total monthly expenditures for all debt obligations.

You'd better shop around

As long as you are going to use credit, you might as well get the best deal you can; rates and terms vary significantly. The reason for your borrowing, the amount you need, your ability to repay, and your creditworthiness will determine whom you can borrow from and the type of loan you can get. Loans fall into two major categories: secured or unsecured. Secured loans use an item, usually your home or car, as collateral. Unsecured debt includes personal loans, lines of credit, and credit cards, and it tends to carry higher interest rates. You might do well to start your expedition by inquiring about the rates and terms at the bank or savings institution where you do your checking and saving. Perhaps you qualify as preferred borrowers and could get a discounted interest rate or lower fees.

The loan of choice these days for homeowners is the home-equity line of credit. Unlike interest on debt that does not use your home or even your vacation home as collateral, interest on home-backed debt is almost always fully deductible up to the price you paid plus improvements. Interest rates on these medium-to-long-term (7 to 20 years) variable rate loans are among the lowest around; rates are usually one to two percentage points over the prime rate. Shop for a lender who might be willing to waive origination fees that could equal 1 to 2 percent of the credit line. Also shop for a loan with the lowest cap on the maximum interest rate you will have to pay.

Home-equity loans make sense if you are going to use the money to remodel your home or pay for school for yourself or your child. But piddling the money away to become a candidate for "Lifestyles of the Rich and Famous" is a big mistake. Fall behind on your payments and you could lose your house. You can generally borrow 80 percent of the current appraised value of your house less your mortgage balance. So if the house you bought five years ago is appraised at $200,000 and your mortgage is $100,000, you would probably be able to borrow $60,000.

Which card in the pack

The key to shopping for credit cards is to get the one that takes your shopping habits into account. If your business requires that you travel and entertain regularly, you will probably want a card such as American Express or Diners Club. Unlike bank cards, the balances on these cards must be paid in full each month and so no interest is incurred. If you are in the market for a bank credit card such as MasterCard or Visa, consider the way you use your card. If you are a so-called revolver (that is, one who makes a minimum payment each month) or if you frequently use your card for cash advances, it will pay to look for a card with a low interest rate. Typical rates in 1989 ran from 14 to 18 percent. If you just use the card for convenience sake and usually pay off the balance each month, then you want a card with a low or no annual fee. Also, make sure that the bank gives you a long grace period, say 25 days, before it starts charging you interest; at some banks interest starts to accrue on the date of sale.

The prestige cards—those heavy-metal versions of Visa, MasterCard, and American Express—cost about 50 percent more in annual fees than their less classy counterparts. Still, there are some advantages. You can often get a higher credit line and special check-cashing privileges that might be a boon if you travel far and frequently. Also, some provide monthly or annual statements that highlight tax-deductible expenses.

No matter how friendly your banker, you are unlikely to find a bank card with low fees *and* low rates. Because of deregulation, you might do better with a card from an out-of-state bank rather than a local one. The Credit Card Locator (Consumer Credit Rating Service, Box 5219, Ocean Park Station, Santa Monica, CA 90405; $10) is a newsletter that lists banks that offer the lowest interest rates and fees and the longest grace periods.

Beyond the limits

Some couples cannot control their debt. They get to the point where they are unable to make their minimum monthly payments and then must borrow even more to make ends meet. They find their financial lives and often their relationship falling apart as creditors put the pressure on. As with any addiction, the

A DEBT-ELIMINATION CALENDAR

Lender:	A____	B____	C____	D____	E____
Month:	Payment:	Payment:	Payment:	Payment:	Payment:
1____	____	____	____	____	____
2____	____	____	____	____	____
3____	____	____	____	____	____
4____	____	____	____	____	____
5____	____	____	____	____	____
6____	____	____	____	____	____
7____	____	____	____	____	____
8____	____	____	____	____	____
9____	____	____	____	____	____
10____	____	____	____	____	____
11____	____	____	____	____	____
12____	____	____	____	____	____
13____	____	____	____	____	____
14____	____	____	____	____	____
15____	____	____	____	____	____
16____	____	____	____	____	____
17____	____	____	____	____	____
18____	____	____	____	____	____
19____	____	____	____	____	____
20____	____	____	____	____	____
21____	____	____	____	____	____
22____	____	____	____	____	____
23____	____	____	____	____	____
24____	____	____	____	____	____

first step to recovery is to admit you are in over your head and immediately stop using credit. If you don't have the willpower to stop borrowing on your own, you might have to cut up your cards and cancel your credit lines. Once you have put a lid on your credit, you can start cutting back so that you can begin to repay your debts.

A debt-elimination calendar can be an enormous help as you develop a pay-back schedule. Take a look at the chart on page 17.

On the Lender line, you can fill in the names of five creditors, putting the creditor you would like to pay off first in the E slot. The lender in slot D should be the one you want paid off next, and so forth. In the Month column, write in the name of the next month after this one and then continue down the column until each month has been listed twice.

Now fill in the hard numbers. Under Payment in column E, list each monthly payment until the loan is paid off. Under Payment in column D, list each payment as long as payments are still being made to creditor E. As soon as creditor E is paid off, add the amount of that payment to the amount being paid to creditor D. This technique, known as "folding over," is continued until all the loans are paid off.

The debt-elimination calendar isn't magic, of course. It will still take self-control to actually make those payments, but at least you have your problem organized and a solution down on paper.

You might find, however, that you just can't manage alone. Fortunately, there are more than 200 nonprofit credit counseling offices around the country that can assist you. You can write to the National Foundation for Consumer Credit (8701 Georgia Avenue, Silver Spring, MD 20910) for the agency in your area. The foundation is sponsored by banks, department stores, and legal groups, among others. You will be requested to fill out a confidential application that will include your income, the amount

Real life, real answers.

At first, Sharon and Peter Davidson had one credit card that hardly had any mileage. But as they settled into their marriage and found that their joint $46,000 income didn't get them too far, the Kansas City couple, both in their early thirties, didn't hesitate to put the card to use. Soon they applied for another card and had no problem getting approved. They used credit for everything—furniture, food, and even cash advances. When they reached the limit on one card, they would simply get another, "just in case." Two years later the Davidsons were on the brink of financial and marital disaster. They owed almost $25,500 on dozens of cards and loans; $4,200 in interest alone. Most of their payments were at least two months behind and the credit cards that had once arrived in the mail were replaced by dunning letters from collection agencies. In desperation, the couple went to a local nonprofit credit counseling service for help.

The credit counselors helped the Davidsons by contacting their creditors and arranging a realistic pay-back schedule. The couple was asked to cut up their cards and alter their lifestyle dramatically. They had to cut back on movies, dining out, and shopping expeditions, hand-launder clothes to avoid cleaning bills, and use a cut-rate phone service. By cutting back they saved $1,000 a month to pay their creditors. The Davidsons, who now pay as they go, can't wait for the day when they are free of debt.

you owe, and to whom you owe it. An initial consultation averages $30. A debt payment plan—costing about $15 a month—requires you to pay a certain percentage of the amount you owe to the agency, which, in turn, pays your creditors.

REDUCING YOUR TAX BILL

We may be in the twenty-first century by the time tax professionals are able to decipher all the provisions of the Tax Reform Act of 1986. What is clear is that tax planning for two-income couples is more important than ever. Perhaps you won't be able to go it alone and will need the help of a financial planner, or at least a savvy accountant to guide you.

For two-career couples, tax reform gave a little, but it took away even more. While it is true that rates are lower (a cap of 28 percent on taxable income replaced the 50 percent top rate), and personal exemptions are higher (from $1,080 in 1986 to $2,000 in 1989), the marriage penalty deduction—in which dual-income married couples were allowed to write off up to $3,000 a year—was abolished. In fact, two-career couples living together unmarried are more likely to get a break than their married counterparts. Two singles filing separate returns pay more of their income tax at the lower 15 percent rate than if they had to combine their incomes—or file separately—as a married couple.

Restricted write-offs

Rather than focus on what you can't do to keep more of your income, focus on the investment and tax-cutting strategies that are available.

Owning a home. A true tax shelter. You can fully deduct mortgage interest and property taxes as well as the interest on a home-equity loan (up to the price you paid plus improvements). Also, if you sell your home, you are allowed to defer the profit on the sale as long as you buy another house within two years that costs as much or more than the one you sold.

Filing separately. If either you or your spouse has high business or medical expenses, you may be able to reduce your bill by filing separate returns. Under the new law, you cannot qualify for a deduction unless your medical expenses, for example, exceed 7.5 percent of your adjusted gross income. If one of you had $5,000 in medical expenses, and together you earned $70,000, you could not take the deduction if you filed jointly. But if you earned $35,000 individually, you would qualify for a

$2,375 write-off, the portion of the $5,000 that exceeds 7.5 percent of $35,000.

Individual Retirement Accounts (IRAs). If you and your spouse are not covered by a corporate pension or profit-sharing plan, you can still deduct up to $2,000 each and put the money into IRAs. Even if you are covered by a company plan, you can claim the entire deduction if your joint adjusted gross income does not exceed $40,000. The amount you can deduct decreases until you earn $50,000, when your contributions are no longer deductible. Even if you cannot deduct the contribution, an IRA is an easy way to get tax-free compounding on the earnings from your investments. You pay taxes only when you withdraw money from your account. If you take cash out before you reach $59^{1}/_{2}$, you will also owe a tax penalty of 10 percent of the money withdrawn.

Keogh Plans. Those who are self-employed, even in a part-time business, can use a Keogh to shelter up to 25 percent of self-employment income or $30,000, whichever is less. Even if you have an IRA, you are allowed to have a Keogh. As with IRAs, your earnings from your investments are tax-free until you take the money out (at $59^{1}/_{2}$ or after). But there is a 10 percent penalty for early withdrawals.

There are several ways to set up a Keogh. The least complicated Keogh is a defined-contribution plan in which you have a fixed, maximum yearly payment. If you choose this type of plan, you have two options. The first is a money-purchase Keogh, in which you must contribute the same percentage every year (up to the smaller of 25 percent or $30,000) unless your business is losing money. The second option is more flexible because you can change your contributions each year. But if you use this option, you can only contribute up to 15 percent of your self-employment income.

Defined-benefit Keoghs are more complicated but make sense for older couples who need to play retirement catch-up. Let's say you are 50 and haven't saved a penny. With a defined-benefit plan, you can save—and deduct—whatever is necessary to let you retire on the average of your highest earnings in three consecutive years; you are not subject to the $30,000/25 percent maximum. You can deduct up to $94,023 if you intend to start making withdrawals at 65. Each year you are required to have an actuary audit your calculations for the IRS.

Simplified Employee Pensions (SEPs). Simplified employee pensions, known as SEPs, are similar to Keoghs. If you have a company with up to 25 employees, you can contribute up to 15 percent a year of each employee's gross income into his or her SEP; your company can take the contribution as a tax deduction. Like an IRA or a Keogh, SEPs can be opened with a bank, brokerage house, or mutual fund. If you pull your money out before you are $59^{1}/_{2}$, you also pay a 10 percent penalty for early withdrawal.

401(k) Plans. These company savings plans, if available to you and your spouse, are a painless way to save. Your contribution is automatically invested so you never have your hands on the money. You do not pay any tax on the earnings until you withdraw the money. Since many companies match all or part of your contribution, that amounts to added tax-deferred earnings. The tax law has restricted once easy withdrawal privileges, however. Now, unless you use the money to pay medical bills, you pay a 10 percent penalty on early withdrawals of your own contributions. The rest is totally off-limits until you retire. Since you are investing pretax dollars, you have, in effect, a tax deduction. If you were in the 28 percent bracket and contributed the maximum allowed to your 401(k) last year ($7,637), you would have reduced your tax bill by $2,135.

Municipal bonds. Municipal bonds (or munis) are issued by state and local governments. The interest, usually paid twice a year, is free from federal taxes and sometimes state and local taxes too if you buy a bond that is issued in your state. Zero coupon municipal bonds are munis that are purchased at a large discount and then are redeemed at a much higher face value later on. You get the tax-free income all at once when you redeem the bond. The most affordable way to have a well-diversified portfolio of munis is through a municipal bond mutual fund or unit trust.

Whole life insurance, universal life insurance, variable life insurance, and variable annuities. These will be explained in more detail in Chapter V, but with all these policies your earnings grow tax-deferred. The tax law has placed no limit on what you can contribute when you buy an annuity or insurance policy. Also, with life insurance you get a death benefit in the bargain.

Limited partnerships. While the tax law eliminated partnerships in which you could deduct more than was invested, low write-off deals are still available. Sold by stockbrokers and financial planners, these programs tend to be real estate partnerships that are not highly leveraged (do not rely on borrowing money). Instead they rely on property depreciation, mortgage interest, and property taxes for tax breaks.

Tax credits for day care. See Chapter IV.

CHOOSING AN ADVISER

Two-career families often have particularly complicated problems involving money. If you earn over $50,000 and have not the time or the inclination to get your own finances in good order, it may make sense to use an adviser to help you manage your two incomes. Here is the cast of characters:

Financial planners

The best financial planners can guide you through the thicket of budgets, investments, insurance, taxes, and retirement planning and help keep you on the path to prosperity. The problem is that too many of the hundred thousand people who call themselves planners are inept. Anyone can hang a shingle and call himself or herself a financial planner. There are no licensing requirements for the profession and no professional group that has the ability to remove the unqualified from the industry. So if you need a planner, you will need to do some homework to find a good one.

First, begin your search with planners who have earned the title Certified Financial Planner (CFP) or Chartered Financial Consultant (ChFC). That means that the planner has passed a series of examinations given by a professional board or an accredited academic institution. While such a title in itself is no guarantee that you have found your financial guru, it is a good place to start. Another positive indicator is membership in the Registry of Financial Planning Practitioners. The men and women in this group, sponsored by the International Association for Financial Planning (IAFP), have been planners for at least three years and have passed a tough, comprehensive examination. You can get a free list of registry members from the IAFP (Suite 800, 2 Concourse Parkway, Atlanta, GA 30328). The Institute of Certified Planners (2 Denver Highlands, 10065 East Harvard Avenue, Suite 320, Denver, CO 80231) also can provide you with a list of local planners.

Find out not only how much the planner is compensated, but also how. Some planners earn their keep by commissions only. Others operate on a fee-plus-commission or fee-only basis. A fee-only planner is totally impartial, but the least common and the most costly, charging $3,000 or more a year.

Unless you use a planner who is compensated only by fees, make sure the planner is willing to justify his or her commissions by explaining how his or her particular recommendations fit into your portfolio. Also make sure that the planner has served other clients of like circumstances. If you are a professional couple, have kids, and earn over six figures, you do not want a planner whose clients are mostly retired people on low fixed incomes.

Evaluate your planner periodically to make sure you are making progress toward reaching your short- and long-term goals.

Money managers

Keeping up with the financial markets is practically a full-time job—at least for professional money managers. If you do not know a blue chip from a greenmail and have considerable assets to invest—at least $100,000—you might want to hire a personal money manager who will put together a portfolio of investments customized to your needs. While there are over 5,000 money managers registered with the U.S. Securities and Exchange Commission, far fewer than that have been top performers. The most important way to evaluate a money manager is by his or her track record; ideally the money manager will have consistently outperformed Standard & Poor's 500-stock index for at least five years. A money manager worth his or her fee— 1 to 2 percent of your balance annually—combines an impressive knowledge of the market with proven results over bad times as well as good.

While a money manager will invest in accordance with your goals, the strategy will be based on his or her own investment philosophy. A growth manager, for example, tries to pick stocks with above-average earnings increases, while those who take the aggressive growth approach usually buy riskier stocks with high price/earnings ratios. Conservative growth managers favor blue chips. Managers who practice market timing cash out when they anticipate a dip in the market while contrarian investors look for value in stocks that other investors have avoided. You should make sure that you understand, and feel comfortable with, your money manager's approach.

Your best chance of finding a first-rate manager is to ask other financial advisers—your lawyer or your accountant, say— for recommendations. Investment advisers must file an ADV form (Uniform Application for Investment Adviser Registration) with the Securities and Exchange Commission. Ask for the manager's ADV Part II, which describes his or her education, work experience, fees, and investment strategy. Also, ask for the names of at least three clients who can give you some personal feedback on the manager's performance.

Certified public accountants

Any tax practitioner can help you complete your tax return. But finding one who can keep more money in your pocket is another matter. Not only do you want your accountant to be well-versed in the ins and outs of tax law—no small task—but you also want a professional who can help you plan your tax strategy throughout the year, not just at the last minute. Again, your best bet in finding such a guiding light is through other financial professionals: your financial planner, lawyer, or some trusted friend or colleague who may have a recommendation.

Using a major national accounting firm is unrealistic; its clientele tends to be corporations and individuals earning $150,000 or more. When you are interviewing accountants, make sure your financial profile is similar to that of others in his or her practice. The more familiarity the accountant has with tax problems of the two-career kind, the better. Accountants' fees depend on how complicated your taxes are as well as where you live. In pricey New York City, hourly fees can go up to $150 an hour, versus maybe $50 an hour in Albuquerque.

Stockbrokers

You cannot buy or sell stocks or bonds without a stockbroker. The trouble is, many are not motivated to do what is right for you. That's because how much they earn is a function of what, and how often, you buy and sell. When brokers push products that carry high commissions or urge frequent trading—whether it is in your interest or not—they make more. Of course, if you do your investing through mutual funds, you do not need a broker at all. If you pick your own stocks and follow the market well enough to know when to ditch a stock, you can pay low commissions and use a discount broker. But if you need someone to recommend what to buy and when to sell, you need a traditional broker.

Since it is just about impossible to verify how well a broker's stock recommendations have done, you must at first rely on recommendations. Be sure that the broker not only knows how to pick stocks, but stays on top of the selections so he or she can quickly advise you when it is time to change gears. Service and accessibility are other key issues. You should have direct access to your broker for critical investment advice. As with money managers, stockbrokers have their own investment approaches which should mesh with your own.

CHAPTER IV

Choosing child care

For two-career couples with children, finding quality child care is critical not only to their children's well-being but to their own as well. If you are constantly worried about the kind of care your child is getting, or frazzled from shuttling your tot from one place one day to another the next, your career and your psyche are bound to suffer. Unfortunately, only one in three couples can count on the traditional solution of grandma or a beloved aunt to help out. The type of child care you choose must be in keeping with your budget as well as with the way you want your kids to be brought up.

EVALUATING YOUR CHILD-CARE NEEDS

☐ What can you realistically afford to pay for child care without cutting back on other activities?

☐ What is the most you can afford to pay for child care if you do cut back on other activities? Which activities or purchases can be trimmed?

☐ Is your family income irregular in any way owing to freelance work, overtime, or business factors? How will this affect your ability to foot the child-care bill on a weekly, monthly, or quarterly basis?

☐ Do you have the kind of job in which you lose money if you stay home with your sick child? What are the financial costs of staying home versus those of paying for child-care arrangements that will work with a sick child?

☐ Do you have access to other affordable help to fill in the gaps in your arrangements—a neighbor, friend, or relative available on short notice and low cost?

- [ ] Do you and your spouse have similar schedules (that is, are both of you gone from nine to five), or overlapping ones (does one of you work weekends, nights, or travel irregularly)? How does this affect your child-care needs? Do you need child care so you can spend time together?
- [ ] How flexible is your work schedule? Do you have expected or unexpected schedule changes such as overtime or late work?
- [ ] Do you or your partner work a shift that precludes certain kinds of day care?
- [ ] How do you and your partner get to work each day? Will your schedules accommodate a trip to the day-care center or baby-sitter?
- [ ] How would a daily sitter get to your house? Are you accessible by public transportation? Would the weather in your area make a sitter's travel to your house unpredictable? Can your schedules accommodate that?

GROUP FACILITIES

Most working parents rely on some form of group care for their children. Group care facilities come in all types and sizes: small private centers; nonprofit groups sponsored by churches, universities, or employers; cooperatives; and large commercial chains such as La Petite Academy and Kinder-Care. Then there are the untold number of facilities that operate in private homes. These day-care homes are mostly unregulated and run by people without professional credentials; yet these people are often experienced mothers who live nearby. Licensing, while it helps to enforce minimum safety, health, and staffing standards, does not guarantee against incompetence or abuse.

Commercial day-care centers usually have the most flexible hours and the most modern facilities. But many commercial centers pay only minimum wage and do not attract the caliber of teacher that nonprofit centers, particularly cooperative ones that allocate a larger part of their budgets to salaries, do. Cooperative day-care centers are an excellent alternative for couples who have time to get involved in the program. Parents, who make up the board of directors, hire teachers, manage finances, set standards, and donate their time—often one day a month—to clean classrooms or act as co-teachers.

CHOOSING ISN'T CHILD'S PLAY

No matter what type of facility you choose, you will have to check it out thoroughly, using the following criteria:

1. Babies need constant cuddling and attention, so make sure there is at least one adult for every three or four babies under two years of age. There should be at least one adult for every five or six toddlers.

2. Group size is important, too. There should be no more than eight children under two in a group, and no more than a dozen toddlers.

3. Teachers should be readily accessible and so should the center itself. While you do not want to interrupt your child's routine, you should be able to show up at any time and feel welcome. You should also be invited in for a formal conference to discuss your child's progress at least twice a year.

4. The center should have plenty of toys and other materials appropriate for your child's age. There should be colorful mobiles, mirrors, and music for infants; lots of books, puzzles, clay, and paint for toddlers; and musical instruments, costumes, and games for preschoolers. There should be a playground nearby if not on the premises so youngsters can get some fresh air and outdoor activity.

5. When you visit the center, check to see that all the children seem engaged and happy. That doesn't mean children shouldn't be given free play time along with organized activities. But you do not want to see children wandering around aimlessly.

6. Check the food. Are both lunches and snacks nutritious and similar to the type of fare your child would get at home? Children should get ample servings and should be able to get seconds if they want them.

7. Make sure that teachers are conscientious about the cleanliness of the facility and your children. Do the staff members wash their hands before and after diapering and feeding babies? Bottles and toothbrushes should be labeled to avoid mix-ups.

8. Procedures should be in place for medical emergencies. The center should have a doctor or nurse on call. Also, parents should be promptly informed about outbreaks of any contagious diseases.

9. The director of the center should be willing to give parents' names as references. Talking to other working parents is one of the best ways to find out about the center.

10. Once you have placed your child in a center, continue to monitor both the facility and your child. While your child may not be ecstatic about leaving mom, he or she should be enthusiastic and happy on a typical day.

Your child's age and the number and credentials of staff usually dictate the cost of group care. If you choose a private school where the majority of the staff have degrees in early childhood education, you can expect to pay up to $700 monthly for infants up to 18 months and $550 for toddlers up to three years. The average cost of care in the United States for children under two is about $400.

ONE-ON-ONE CARE

For many affluent two-career couples, the option of choice is a nanny—one woman who cares for your child or children in your own home. If you choose well, the benefits of one-on-one care for your child are many. Your child will have the attention, cuddling, and care he or she needs throughout the day and will have a strong, loving relationship with the caregiver. But finding a Mary Poppins won't be easy or cheap. One of the best ways to find a nanny or au pair is through neighborhood networking. You ask around and you hear that the Gordons will soon be letting Janet go because they're moving to Chattanooga. She's been with them for three years and she's a treasure. Grab her.

Other sources for finding a caregiver include local or ethnic newspapers in which candidates advertise; local parenting newspapers that are passed out in pediatricians' offices and children's stores; and a growing number of employment agencies that cater to the housekeeping and nanny set. Agencies are pricey; expect to pay as much as a month's wages in fees. Those monthly wages could add up to a whopping $1,200 for a 45-hour week for an experienced helper with her citizenship papers or her green card. If you are looking for live-in help and can provide room and board, you can expect to pay less. Agencies will do most of the screening for you. Tell them your prerequisites—for example, a nonsmoking older woman with a grown family who drives a car—and they will do the rest, including checking references.

CHOOSING AN AGENCY

If you are going to rely on an employment agency, it should be a good one. Take time to interview the director; let the following questions guide you.

1. Where do you get your applicants? Find out if they are local candidates or people who have been recruited from out of town. If the agency places non-U.S. citizens, ask if these women have their green cards. Does the agency get referrals from other women it has placed? Ask if you can be given the names and phone numbers of some of its clients. An agency that gets referrals from both the applicants and the clients is obviously doing something right.

2. What level of experience do your applicants have? If you are looking for an older woman with years of experience, or a professional nanny, do not waste your time going to see an agency that only places young women from the Midwest. Find out exactly what types of helpers it supplies.

3. What is the salary range that your applicants expect? Asking this simple question in advance can save you a lot of time. If the candidates are getting $250 a week and up and you cannot pay more than $150, you need to find another agency.

4. What is your fee? All employment agencies charge a fee, payable by you; this is how they make their money. But policies differ. Some agencies charge a flat fee, ranging from a low of $400 to a high of $900. Others base the fee on the salary. The charge may vary; the possibilities include the equivalent of two weeks' or one month's salary, or 10 percent of a year's salary. In some cases you will be asked to pay a retainer fee, which will be applied to the placement fee once a nanny is hired. If you do not hire one of the agency's candidates, however, the retainer fee probably will not be refunded.

5. How do you select the applicants you represent? You have standards and you want the agency you are dealing with to have some, too. One Connecticut agency, for example, requires that all applicants be at least 18, have a high school diploma, be able to swim, have a valid driver's license with a clean driving record, and have at least three child-related references. The best agencies turn away more applicants than they represent. The usual figure is one applicant accepted out of every three or four.

6. Do you personally interview the applicants? The answer may seem self-evident, but it is not. There are a number of agencies that recruit young women from out of state but never meet them in person. They do, of course, check references and interview them by phone, but you may not feel comfortable with this procedure. Some of the agencies that follow this practice have been very successful with their placements and enjoy good reputations.

7. Are you licensed? Many states require that, for the protection of the consumer, employment agencies be licensed by the state department of labor. Getting a license normally requires the payment of a fee—about $150—per year; the filing of some paperwork, including such items as references and all forms and documents that will be used to conduct business; the purchase of a surety bond; and, in some states, the fulfillment of certain physical requirements for office space. This last requirement can be difficult for operators of small businesses and those just starting out.

If an agency that interests you is not licensed (and we talked to some directors of unlicensed agencies who were as thorough and intelligent as their licensed colleagues), ask why. You may find the reasons to be satisfactory .

Regardless of whether the agency is licensed, there is one more thing you can do to assure yourself that you are dealing with a reputable business. Call your local Better Business Bureau or Consumer Affairs Department to find out whether there have been any complaints against the agency that you are considering. If you find that there have been a number of complaints or any serious charges, you are obviously going to look for another agency.

8. Are you bonded? If an agency is licensed, it probably had to put up a surety bond that would be forfeited if it were to not fulfill its obligations properly. In some cases the applicants will be bonded as well.

You might also ask if the agency does a criminal check on its applicants, and whether such a check is made through the local police or through the FBI. One agency in Minnesota that conducts an FBI check found that one of its candidates had recently been released from an Illinois prison, where she had been serving time for child molestation. Some agencies will run such a check only if you request it, so it is certainly worth asking about.

9. Will you replace a nanny who doesn't work out? Again, policies differ. The best guarantee is an agency that will replace a nanny or mother's helper anytime within the first four months. A 30-day guarantee is more typical, however, and you should not work with an agency that does not offer at least that.

Remember, though, if the woman you have hired leaves for "cause," you won't get a nickel back or another placement from most agencies. "Cause" might be something as serious as physical abuse or something as seemingly simple as asking the woman to do more work than you originally agreed to. That's why agencies recommend, and many require, a written agreement specifying duties, wages, and method of payment.

WHAT TO ASK A PROSPECTIVE NANNY

Once you have a few candidates, invite each to your home for an interview. Have each one meet your child and, if at all possible, your spouse. Describe the job and then take some time to get to know each candidate. You want to like the person who will be spending so much time with your child. Ask questions:

☐ Why do you want to be a nanny?

☐ Do you have any children? How old? What are they doing now?

☐ Have you ever been away from home before? For how long and under what circumstances? How do you feel about leaving home? Do you think you might get homesick? (For live-in nannies.)

☐ Tell me about your previous jobs. What did you like and not like about them? Why did you leave them? How long did you work there?

☐ Tell me about your experiences with young children. What was the worst experience you ever had babysitting? What did you enjoy most? What kinds of things did you like to do with the children you sat for?

- [ ] Tell me about your family. Do you have brothers and sisters? What are they doing now? Were your parents very strict with you? If you did something wrong, how were you punished? Do you think you will do things differently with your own children or bring them up in much the same way?
- [ ] Tell me about your high school or college. What were your favorite subjects? What activities were you involved in?
- [ ] Are you a licensed driver? For how long? Have you ever gotten a speeding ticket or other moving violation?
- [ ] Do you have any experience taking care of pets? Do you have any allergies to animals? Would you mind helping to take care of our pet(s)?
- [ ] Do you smoke? Will it bother you if we do?
- [ ] Do you drink? Will it bother you if we do?
- [ ] Have you ever used any drugs?
- [ ] Have you ever been arrested?
- [ ] Have you had a physical examination in the last year? May we see the results? (Many agencies require this; you might want to as well.)
- [ ] Whom can we call as references, and how do you know them? (The agency should provide these.) At least one reference should be child-care-related. Ask your reference whether he or she would hire her again.

Hiring a foreign worker

You can expect to pay a lot less if you hire a non-U.S. citizen without a green card (permanent legal status) or if you "import" a nanny on a tourist visa. Keep in mind, though, that you are risking a lot if you hire either type of illegal alien. Not only is she breaking the law by working here, you are breaking the law as well for hiring her.

There are, however, some government-authorized programs that place young English-speaking Europeans with American families for one year. Each au pair lives in the home as a family member who is available to help with child care and light housekeeping. For more information contact Au Pair Homestay USA, 1411 K Street, N.W., Washington, D.C. 20005:

(202) 628-7134; or Au Pair in America, American Institute for Foreign Study, 102 Greenwich Avenue, Greenwich, CT 06830: (203) 869-9090.

The parent as employer

It is possible that when you hire your nanny you will be an employer for the first time. If that's the case, you will probably have plenty of questions about the financial and legal obligations you are about to incur. How do I decide how much vacation she gets? Is it wise to pay my caregiver off the books? What taxes will I have to pay? What benefits should I offer?

Many parents—even those who negotiate contracts at work with ease—find ironing out similar agreements with their nanny time-consuming, embarrassing, or even trifling. But a clear financial arrangement made at the outset, establishing the time commitment, wages, precise responsibilities of both parties, and type of benefits you will provide, will pave the way for a smooth relationship.

The war over wages

According to the Fair Labor Standards Act of 1982, any caregiver whose work exceeds 20 hours a week is considered full-time and by law must be paid the minimum wage (now $3.35 an hour). Though live-in caregivers are subject to the minimum wage act, they are not covered under the Fair Labor Standards Act with provisions for overtime. It is generally agreed that it is difficult to determine how many hours they work since their workplace is also their home. Whether live-in or live-out, you should expect your nanny to work 40 to 45 hours a week.

Pay rates for nannies generally fall into three levels. A beginner is probably someone new in the country with little or no English-language skills or paid child-care experience. The pay rate for these mother's helpers or au pairs is between $125 and $150 per week. At the next level, the person may have two or more years' experience but be only moderately fluent in English. Standard pay for those at the intermediate level is from $150 to $200. Any child-care worker with over five years' paid experience, or any person who has completed specialized training, such as attending a nanny school, is categorized as a professional. The pay rate for a professional nanny ranges from $200 to $300 or more per week. Of course, there are other, extenuating factors to consider, such as the going rate for your particular area, extra duties that will be required in addition to child care, and the number of children under the nanny's care.

The taxes you can expect to pay for your live-in helper will add a thousand dollars or more to your total child-care tab. To expedite matters and lessen your burden at tax time, be sure to keep good records. Apply to the U.S. Internal Revenue Service for a federal employer identification number (EIN). At the same time, request the *Employer's Tax Guide*, which you will find packed with helpful information for the first-time employer. To make state-related deductions, you will also need to apply for a state employer identification number. Plan to contend with four types of taxes: Social Security (FICA), withholding, unemployment insurance, and workers' compensation.

Make sure you specify the method of payment before you hire a nanny. More than one employer has been caught up in the difficult situation of presenting a check to a household employee who was expecting cash. Also make clear how often you intend to pay your helper. The usual pay period is once a week; should you decide to pay monthly, remember that a month is 4.3 weeks.

If you are hiring a live-in caretaker, expect to give her two days off per week, either split up or back to back. The number of sick days, paid holidays, and vacation time can vary. Typically, nannies get four to six sick days per year, one week of paid vacation after the first year of employment, and two weeks after two or more years. You should decide in advance if you expect your nanny's vacation time to coincide with your own or if you'd prefer that she accompany you on your holiday and take hers

Real life, real answers.

Janice and Carl Spiro of Camden, Maine, hired a mother's helper and, at her insistence, paid her off the books. During this time the girl invited her boyfriend over to tour the house during a dinner party, spent one full afternoon napping, and was an hour late picking the children up from school. An unhappy Janice Spiro fired the girl, assuming that she had seen the worst and the last of the situation. But her indignant former employee sued for severance pay and minimum wage violation. It became a nightmare of entanglements with the labor board. As the Spiros calculated it, considering the time the girl had actually worked, she had been paid handsomely—well above the minimum wage—but they had no written agreement or canceled checks.

at another time. Give six to eight paid holidays per year and make the dates specific. Do not be unexpectedly left in the lurch New Year's Eve, or find out that you have an unhappy conscript for Thanksgiving.

On the books or off

To some couples, under-the-table cash payments are a great temptation when faced with the extra costs and forms required by the government. But not only are off-the-book payments illegal, they probably won't save you much money in the long run. What's more, there may be hidden bombshells in paying a live-in caregiver unreported cash. Even if your employee begs to be paid off the books, when culpability is assessed, it is your responsibility to follow the guidelines for minimum wages and taxes.

Get it in writing

A contract can relieve a lot of the emotional difficulties of hiring someone to work in your home, freeing both sides from guilt, defensiveness, or resentment. A good contract will make both you and your helper aware of each other's rights and responsibilities. It should detail everything that can reasonably be specified; other areas of concern that cannot be spelled out in writing can at least be discussed verbally.

The contract should include most, if not all, of the following types of information.

- [ ] The date.
- [ ] The full name of your employee.
- [ ] Her Social Security number.
- [ ] Your full name.
- [ ] Your address.
- [ ] The names of your children.
- [ ] The length of her commitment.
- [ ] Her basic salary.
- [ ] Any overtime provisions.
- [ ] Her days off.
- [ ] All vacation, sick days, holidays.
- [ ] The method and frequency of payment.
- [ ] Provisions for taxes, workers' compensation, disability, and unemployment insurance.
- [ ] Medical insurance and other benefits.
- [ ] Your salary review policy.
- [ ] Her specific household duties, other than child care, and the number of times per week they are to be done.
- [ ] Use of car/auto insurance.
- [ ] Living conditions (for live-ins).
- [ ] Curfews (for live-ins).
- [ ] Telephone policy (for live-ins).
- [ ] Guest policy (for live-ins).
- [ ] Provisions for return travel payment or reimbursement (for live-ins).
- [ ] Reasons for termination of employment.

The format of the contract is unimportant; it might be a list or a letter—formal or informal—whatever you and she are most comfortable with. Just make certain that both of you sign the agreement and that each of you keeps a copy. This document, and the respect that it implies, is the key to establishing and maintaining a good relationship.

TAX BREAKS

Fortunately, there are tax breaks to help offset the cost of child care. First, make sure you claim the exemption for dependents on your tax return—$2,000 per child in 1989. Then, you may also be eligible for a tax credit for your day-care expenses. The credit—a dollar-for-dollar reduction of your tax bill—is a percentage of the first $2,400 of expenses for one dependent child and the first $4,800 for two or more children. Depending on your income, you can claim a credit of as much as $720 if you have one child and $1,440 if you have two or more. To qualify for the credit, your day-care costs must be paid to someone who is not your dependent (your mother, for instance) who provides care in your home, or to a day-care facility caring for more than six children. Your children must be under 15 and you must be working, looking for a job, or attending school full-time to claim the credit.

If you or your spouse work for a company that offers a dependent-care flexible spending account (FSA), you may be able to get an even bigger tax break. Such accounts allow employees to use pretax dollars to pay for day care. The limit is typically $5,000 a year. However, you must decide before the beginning of each year how much money to put in the account. You cannot recover what you do not spend. Also, every dollar that you spend from your spending account reduces by $1 the day-care expenses that qualify for a tax credit. So while you could technically use both your FSA and the credit to reduce your expenses, you must, for all practical purposes, choose between them.

A TAX CREDIT CHECKLIST

To determine whether or not you are eligible for a tax credit on child-care expenses, go over these rules:

- [ ] Both you and your spouse must be gainfully employed, looking for work, or attending school full-time.
- [ ] Your dependents must be under 15.
- [ ] You must be paying at least half the cost of maintaining your household.
- [ ] You must keep records of all your expenses related to child care and of all wages paid.
- [ ] You must make the necessary payroll deductions and pay the unemployment taxes.
- [ ] Your child-care employee must furnish you with a Social Security account number.
- [ ] You must record wages paid to your caregiver for duties other than direct dependent care, such as cooking, cleaning, or driving.

Payments for child care are determined by a sliding scale. The top credit for child care is currently $720 for one child and $1,140 for two or more. A number of factors determine the actual amount of your credit—your income, the amount of your child-care expenses, and the number of qualifying children.

CHAPTER V

The assurance of insurance

A s a two-career couple you have both been working hard toward achieving your financial goals. Chances are you never think about what would happen to you and your family if everything came unraveled. But what if the unthinkable were to happen tomorrow? A continuing survey by the University of Michigan has shown that in any decade, three out of four American families are likely to suffer a serious threat to their economic well-being, such as a layoff, a disabling illness, divorce, or widowhood.

While you cannot insure against the loss of a job or the failure of a marriage, you should, depending on your family circumstances, have life, health, disability, and homeowners policies to protect all that you have worked so hard to attain. That does not mean you should weigh yourself down with insurance that you won't need. Rather, get the most complete coverage you can but do not spend money insuring yourself against a loss that you could afford to take care of on your own.

COORDINATING COMPANY BENEFITS

The first thing you want to do as a two-career couple is to coordinate your company benefits to make sure your family is adequately but not overly insured, particularly if you are paying for benefits from your own pockets. Most companies are not as generous about footing the bill as they once were. As insurance costs soar and a growing number of corporations demand that employees share the burden of rising premiums, it makes sense to compare your benefits.

At the same time employers are asking employees to pick up a greater part of the tab, many are giving employees more of a choice about how comprehensive they want their coverage to be with so-called flexible benefit plans. You may be able to pick out the most complete, most affordable parts of each plan, say health and dental from one package and life and disability from another. Choose the health plan that offers more generous benefits, or that pays the hospital directly, rather than the policy that reimburses you after you have laid out the cash. If your spouse's plan provides adequate and inexpensive—or free— insurance for the whole family, opt for the least comprehensive coverage in your own plan. If your employer is paying for an essentially inactive health policy, you might as well keep it. While you won't be able to collect double, one may pick up where the other leaves off. If you are paying for coverage you do not need, ask your benefits office if you can refuse medical coverage entirely; this can save you up to $1,000 a year.

Of course, some couples may still find some parts of their group coverage woefully inadequate or even nonexistent, es- pecially if they are self-employed or work for a small company. Others may want to beef up their life insurance coverage, for example, as a way to build up their assets tax-deferred. The major areas of insurance and ways to evaluate your coverage follow.

LIFE INSURANCE

Nothing about life insurance these days is easy, neither how much you need nor what kind to buy. If you are a couple without children and each of you would be self-supporting if alone, life insurance is optional. If you have or are about to start a family,

Real life, real answers.

T ara and Daniel O'Connor waited until their son, Timmy, was eight before they woke up to the fact that they'd better augment their life insurance coverage, then consisting of a $25,000 policy for each. First they estimated what their current needs would be if one of them died: $5,000 in funeral costs; $5,000 in bills; another $3,000 for legal fees associated with the death. Then they added $150,000 in income needs, $80,000 for college for Timmy, and $150,000 to pay off their mortgage, for a total of $393,000. They reduced this amount by their $145,000 in assets, including the equity in their home, vested pension plans, and their savings and investments. Each one needed $248,000 in life insurance. (See chart on page 47.)

it is critical. If one of you has health problems or you have been unable to save very much, your needs will be greater.

Basically, a family's life insurance should cover any immediate expenses following a death, such as funeral costs, outstanding bills, and legal fees. Then add income needs—roughly 70 to 80 percent of the family's current total after-tax income, multiplied by the number of years until the youngest child turns 18. Also factor in a college education for each of your children (about $80,000 for four years at a public university in 10 years, at least twice that for a private school). You may want to include the balance of your mortgage and other expenses you would like to have paid off if one of you were to die prematurely. Then calculate the total value of your current assets. The difference between what you will have accumulated in assets and what you will need is the amount of your insurance requirement.

You will find no end of companies or agents willing to help you meet your insurance needs. But you want to look only at policies from financially viable insurance companies—those likely to outlive you. The insurer should have an A or A+ rating for at least 10 years from A.M. Best & Company, the independent insurance rating service. Your agent or local library should have a current copy of the Best rating list. The cost of your policy will depend on several variables: your age, your sex (women pay less because they live longer), your health, whether or not you smoke, and, of course, the type of policy you choose.

Annual renewable term life insurance used to be the protection of choice; it was simple to understand, flexible, and, depending on your age, cheap. But financial advisers have reevaluated the merits of other types of policies, such as whole life, variable life, and universal life, since the earnings on these policies are tax-deferred until the money is withdrawn. Here are your life insurance options:

Term insurance

There is no icing on this cake. You buy a policy that provides a specific amount of term insurance and your beneficiary receives that amount when you die. The term of the policy is usually one year. While the premium does not vary during the term of the policy, it does go up when you renew each term— as you get older. If you are buying term insurance, insist on annual renewable policies that guarantee you can renew automatically without a physical exam. Also, try to buy convertible term policy, which lets you switch over to a whole life or universal life policy at a specific point in time. The cost of term insurance varies, but you might pay about $325 a year for a $200,000 policy at age 35, and $550 for the same policy at 40.

Whole life insurance

The premiums you pay for a whole life policy buy two benefits. One is the death benefit. The other is a savings element, or cash value. The cash value increases each year, not only because you have paid more premiums, but because the policy offers a guaranteed interest rate and the company pays annual dividends. The interest and dividends are not taxable, so your money compounds tax-free. A 35-year-old man who buys

HOW MUCH LIFE INSURANCE DO YOU NEED?

Income needs		O'Connors	Your family
1. Funeral		$5,000	_____
2. Legal and other expenses	+	3,000	_____
3. Pay off mortgage (optional)	+	150,000	_____
4. Pay off other debts (optional)	+	5,000	_____
5. College fund per child	+	80,000	_____
6. Living expenses:			
Your current living expenses	50,000		_____
x 80%	40,000		_____
– Your spouse's take-home pay	25,000		_____
= Annual need	15,000		_____
x Number of years needed (10)	=150,000 +	150,000	_____
	Total (a)	$393,000	_____

Assets

		O'Connors	Your family
1. Home equity		$110,000	_____
2. Other equity		_____	_____
3. Pension plan		15,000	_____
4. Stocks and bonds		_____	_____
5. Other savings		20,000	_____
	Total (b)	$145,000	_____

Life insurance needs

		O'Connors	Your family
Total (a)		$393,000	_____
Minus total (b)		145,000	_____
Coverage needed		$248,000	_____

$200,000 worth of insurance might spend $2,500 for whole life versus $325 for term. But while the price of term increases annually, whole life stays the same. Policyholders can borrow an amount equal to what they would get if they cashed in the policy and pay it back at their convenience. Interest rates, however, are not as attractive as they once were: expect to pay a fixed rate of 8 percent or so.

Variable life insurance

This is an alternative for two-career couples who want insurance and are not averse to taking risks for a potentially larger cash value and death benefit. With variable life, you decide how your premiums are invested—in stocks, bonds, or money market portfolios resembling mutual funds. You can switch among them by writing to (or with some companies, phoning) the insurer. While you can accumulate a hefty sum if your investments do well, your cash value can take a dive if your investments do poorly. The death benefit, however, can never drop below the face amount of the policy.

Universal life insurance

Universal life was built for flexibility. You can vary your coverage, investments, and premiums, increasing them or reducing them from time to time if you are in a pinch. You can even skip an occasional premium and pay your insurance out of the policy's investments. You are told the current rate of return on your cash value before expenses and the part of your premium that is paying for company costs. Universal is also less costly than whole life; about a third less for the same death benefit.

HEALTH INSURANCE

If you are not covered by a group major medical program by one of your employers, the most important checkup you can have these days is a self-examination of your health insurance to make sure you have adequate and reliable coverage. Not

HOW PERMANENT POLICIES DIFFER

	Policy provides	Values to policyholder	Death benefits
Traditional whole life	Fixed premium payments but can borrow on cash values to pay Guaranteed cash values	Policyholder can borrow against cash value/ dividends or withdraw dividends Dividends can be paid in cash, can reduce premiums, or can buy more paid-up insurance	Guaranteed death benefit which can increase from dividends purchasing paid-up insurance
Universal life	Policyholder can adjust premiums Cash values vary with interest rate performance	Insurance company invests cash value at a current interest rate, but policy provides for a minimum rate of return Policyholder can borrow against or make partial withdrawals	Guaranteed minimum death benefit, but can otherwise be varied by policyholder
Variable life	Fixed premium payment but can borrow on cash values to pay Cash values vary with fund performance with risk to policyholder	Policyholder chooses from various funds to invest cash values Policyholder can borrow against cash values Generally no interest rate guarantees	Variable, but not lower than original face amount of policy
Variable universal life	Policyholder can vary premium amounts paid Cash values vary with fund performance	Policyholder chooses investment fund to invest cash values Policyholder can borrow against cash values or make withdrawals Interest rate varies with fund performance	Guaranteed minimum death benefit, not lower than the original face amount of the policy Policyholder can vary death benefit, which may also vary with fund performance

having the protection you need could be an immediate threat to your family's financial well-being. Consider that a coronary by-pass costs $25,000 and a kidney transplant upwards of $75,000. If you are planning on having a family, consider how much you would have to spend without insurance. Your bundle of joy will cost a bundle. Routine hospital and delivery fees average $2,500; add another $1,500 for a caesarean.

The most comprehensive type of coverage is available through a major medical policy, which you can get from private health companies as well as the Blue Cross/Blue Shield network. The optimal plan has a low deductible but limits your out-of-pocket expenses to $1,000 a year—100 percent is paid after that; has a $1 million or higher ceiling on the amount of lifetime coverage; and includes psychiatric and home health care. The policy should also be guaranteed renewable; that is, as long as you pay your premiums, the insurer cannot cancel the policy. Such a paragon policy is hard to get and costly if you are not covered by a group plan. Your best bet in finding such a policy is to use an independent insurance agent who represents several companies, giving you a choice. Local chapters of the National Association of Life Underwriters (1922 F Street, N.W., Washington, DC 20006) will supply names of reputable agents. Expect to pay at least $4,500 a year for a comprehensive family policy.

Another alternative is to look into getting group insurance through some affiliation other than your job. Association plans, which come close to matching top-notch company plans and may be cheaper than individual coverage, may be sponsored by your professional society, college alumni association, labor union, religious group, or some other association.

Another possibility is joining a Health Maintenance Organization (HMO). About half of the nation's 750 HMOs accept nongroup participants. The average up-front cost—$2,500 for a family—may be about the same as a premium for standard health insurance, but your out-of-pocket expenses will be minimal. If you go the HMO route, make sure your HMO is federally qualified and that at least 60 percent of its doctors are board certified.

DISABILITY

Disability is frequently overlooked by young couples. It shouldn't be. A 32-year-old male, for example, runs a six and a half times greater risk of being disabled for three months or longer than he does of dying during his working years. Almost everyone has the disability insurance provided by Social Security. But the maximum benefit, around $1,300 a month, is not likely to meet your needs. And such benefits may be denied unless you can prove that you will not be able to engage in any gainful employment for at least a year. Even then, it takes six months before the checks start rolling in.

First you will need to find out how much disability coverage you have, probably from your company. William and Catherine O'Hara of San Francisco discovered unexpected coverage when William broke his leg in an automobile accident. His auto insurance paid him $850 a month for a year and a $5,000 bank loan included disability insurance equal to the monthly payments until the debt was paid. Ideally, your total disability coverage should replace close to 70 percent of your pretax income. If you have to buy the insurance on your own, a worthwhile policy may cost at least $1,000 a year, or as much as $4,000, depending on the coverage.

With the help of an insurance agent, choose a policy by comparing the costs, the size of the deductible, and the benefits. Also use the following features as your guide:

Waiting period. This is the time from when you first become sick or injured to the time when you begin to receive benefits. You can save several hundred dollars on your premium by choosing a policy with a longer waiting period. If you have an

DISABILITY POLICY COMPARISON CHECKLIST

Feature	Recommendation	Policy 1	Policy 2	Policy 3
Waiting period	2–3 months	_____	_____	_____
Definition of disability	Own occupation if possible	_____	_____	_____
Length of benefits	Until 65	_____	_____	_____
Renewability	Guaranteed	_____	_____	_____
Options				
_____		_____	_____	_____
_____		_____	_____	_____
_____		_____	_____	_____
Annual premium		_____	_____	_____

emergency reserve to turn to, choose a policy with a two-month or three-month waiting period.

Coverage. Some policies restrict coverage to those who are permanently disabled and are unable to do any work. Some policies cover illness or injury but not both. You should shop for the most liberal coverage you can afford, one that will provide benefits if you are unable to pursue your own occupation whether from illness or injury.

Length of benefits. Your coverage should continue until you are 65 if you are permanently disabled. Some companies offer policies with residual benefits. That means that if you are able to return to work part-time, the company will continue to pay partial benefits based on your lost income.

Renewability. The best policies are noncancelable and

guaranteed renewable until age 65. This freezes the premium at its original premium price for as long as you make the premium payments.

HOMEOWNERS INSURANCE

Most homeowners have invested so much of their savings into their dwelling and its contents that they probably would face financial ruin if something were to destroy it. That's where homeowners policies come in. The policy you buy should protect you against any damage to, or theft of, your real estate or personal property. It also should afford liability protection in case of accidents that occur on your property or elsewhere.

The insurance industry has a standard ranking of types of policies. The policy that is most commonly recommended is known as HO-3, or "open peril" coverage. It covers everything except what the policy specifically states it excludes—usually earthquakes, floods (you should have special flood insurance if you live in a flood zone), termites, and rodents. An HO-5 is the king of home policies. It has the same general coverage as HO-3 except that the contents of your home and your personal property are covered for much higher amounts. Owners of condominiums and cooperatives should look into HO-6 policies, and renters can get insurance in the form of HO-4 policies. If you operate a business at home you can get a special policy that offers additional property and liability coverage.

The amount of insurance you have should be based on what it would cost to rebuild your home—not on its market value, which may be more or less than replacement cost. Your coverage should be at least 80 percent of the actual cost of rebuilding your home if it is damaged or destroyed.

The standard liability amount in a homeowners policy is $100,000. But for an extra $15 or so a year, you can raise the coverage to $300,000. Neither homeowners liability nor automobile liability will protect you from non-accident-related suits

THE 80% RULE FOR HOMEOWNERS LOSS SETTLEMENT

	Partial loss	Total loss
If house is insured to at least 80% of replacement cost	Full replacement	Full replacement (up to amount of policy)
If house is not insured to at least 80% of replacement cost	Depreciated value (actual cash value)	Depreciated value (actual cash value)

Depreciated value = Replacement cost less physical depreciation, calculated by your insurance company.

---

such as libel, slander, or invasion of privacy. An umbrella liability policy offers such coverage.

AUTOMOBILE INSURANCE

If you own a car, you own automobile insurance. One reason is that most states require licensed drivers who own an automobile to carry liability insurance. Also, if you are inadequately insured and have an accident, the losses could be devastating financially as well as physically.

There are four types of coverage in an automobile insurance policy. Liability insurance protects you if you are sued, whether or not the accident was your fault. Your limit on bodily injury liability should be at least 100/300 ($100,000 per person up to a maximum of $300,000 per accident); limits on property damage should be at least 25/50. Medical payments coverage is for medical expenses for you and your passengers. Even if you already have health insurance—and you should—you should carry about $10,000 worth of this coverage.

The third part of your auto package is uninsured motorist protection. This covers you and your passengers if you are injured by a driver who has no insurance. The amount, which covers bodily injury only, should be at least 100/300. Finally, you probably want to be covered for property damage. This

AUTO INSURANCE POLICY COMPARISON CHECKLIST

Feature	Recommendation	Policy 1	Policy 2	Policy 3
Bodily injury liability	$100,000/300,000	_____	_____	_____
Property damage	$25,000/50,000	_____	_____	_____
Medical payments	$10,000	_____	_____	_____
Uninsured/ underinsured motorist	$100,000/300,000	_____	_____	_____
Collision	Highest deductible you can handle	_____	_____	_____
Comprehensive	Highest deductible you can handle	_____	_____	_____
Options	_____	_____	_____	_____
	_____	_____	_____	_____
Premium		_____	_____	_____

includes collision coverage, damage to your car when you have collided with any object, and comprehensive coverage, your main protection against theft and vandalism. Your deductibles on collision and comprehensive should be the highest you can afford. But once the premium for that portion of your insurance is 10 percent or more of the car's value, or if your car is more than five years old (not counting classic models), you might want to consider discontinuing it altogether.

YOUR INSURANCE INVENTORY

Type	Carrier	Amount	Deductible	Annual premium	Notes
Life	____	____	_____	_____	___
Health	____	____	_____	_____	___
Disability	____	____	_____	_____	___
Homeowners	____	____	_____	_____	___
Car	____	____	_____	_____	___
Other	____	____	_____	_____	___

UNNECESSARY INSURANCE

With so many critical insurance needs, it is hard to imagine a couple wanting to buy insurance they do not need. If you are adequately covered with life insurance as outlined above, there is no reason to be tempted by flight insurance, loan or mortgage insurance—or insurance on the life of your children. The narrower the coverage, the less economical the policy is likely to be. By the same token, if you have ample health coverage, avoid cancer insurance or hospital insurance by the day; these policies are often pitched over television in the wee hours, when you are at your most vulnerable.

CHAPTER VI

Accumulating for college

Saving for college is like learning a foreign language: the earlier in life you start, the easier it is. Funding college is the second biggest investment most couples make, after buying a home. Indeed, if your toddler eventually toddles off to Harvard or some other Ivy League college where tuition, room, and board may well tote up to $150,000 within a few years, it may even be your biggest investment. For many young couples, saving for a newborn child's college expenses is like planning for their own retirement; they can't even imagine it. The important thing, however, is to begin some sort of systematic savings plan.

To do that you will need to figure out how much money to put away and when. How much you need depends on the type of school your child is likely to attend. A college education now costs an average of $10,000 a year, probably twice that at Ivy League or other top private schools. Figure that the bill is likely to bounce 6 to 7 percent a year. Depending on how many years you have to go until your child enters college, increase the current costs by the appropriate amount. Then calculate how much you'd need to save each year assuming your funds can earn a respectable 8 percent return. If, for example, you have a newborn, you would have to put away about $3,600 a year to

A COLLEGE FINANCIAL PLANNER

What 1 year of college will cost: 7% inflation	Years until your child enters college	Yearly investment required: 8% return	Yearly investment required: 12 % return
$10,700	1	$9,907	$9,554
11,449	2	5,504	5,400
12,250	3	3,773	3,630
13,108	4	2,909	2,743
14,026	5	2,391	2,208
15,007	6	2,046	1,849
16,058	7	1,800	1,592
17,182	8	1,615	1,397
18,385	9	1,472	1,244
19,672	10	1,358	1,121
21,049	11	1,265	1,019
22,522	12	1,187	933
24,098	13	1,121	860
25,785	14	1,065	796
27,590	15	1,016	740
29,522	16	974	691
31,588	17	936	646
33,799	18	903	606

Note: Assumes that the cost of one year in college today is $10,000 and that the annual inflation of college costs will be 7 percent. The returns shown are after tax.

pay for his or her B.A. If you have a 12 year old, you would have to more than double that amount.

PASSING THE BUCKS

Before tax reform, the government gave beleaguered parents a break, allowing them to cut taxes by transferring assets to their children through gifts and trusts. The income from the investments was then taxed at the child's considerably lower rate. Today you will find Uncle Sam less avuncular. Parents have been hit with a double whammy. They have fewer opportunities to shift assets and fewer tax advantages when they do.

Indeed, with tax reform came a provision dubbed the kiddie tax. Now any interest, dividends, or other investment income over $1,000 earned by a child under 14 is taxed at his or her parents' rate. At age 14 a child goes through an economic rite of passage and any such unearned income above $500 but less than $17,850 is taxed at the child's rate, usually15 percent. Besides the tax increases, reform also toughened the rules on short-term trusts such as the Clifford, much touted because the earnings were taxed at the child's rate and the assets accumulated for 10 years and then reverted back to the parents. None of the trusts that survived reform have such advantages.

While asset shifting has been undermined by tax reform, there are alternative ways for parents to keep more money in the family through a combination of well-timed gifts to children and tax-deferred and tax-exempt investments. While lower tax rates for parents—and higher ones for children—have made shifting assets less compelling than before tax reform, there are still tax advantages to asset shifting. You can continue to give a child up to $10,000 a year ($20,000 with your spouse) without paying a gift tax. Even with a hefty return of 10 percent, a child under 14 can still have assets of $10,000 and not be taxed at his or her parents' rate (the first $500 isn't taxed; the next $500 is taxed at 15 percent). If your child is 14 or older, he or she can earn as much as $17,850 before being pushed above the 15 percent bracket.

UGMAs OR UTMAs

The easiest way to give money to a child under 18 is to set up a custodial account under the Uniform Gift to Minors Act (UGMA) or, depending on the state you live in, its newer sibling, the Uniform Transfer to Minors Act (UTMA). These accounts, which can be set up through a banker or broker, are inexpensive techniques to transfer assets to a minor without the necessity of any monitoring by the courts.

These accounts, especially the UGMA, do have drawbacks, however. Under a UGMA, parents are limited to gifts of cash or securities. Also, the assets automatically go to your child when he or she turns 18. If your child would rather buy a BMW than a B.A., that's his or her choice. With a UTMA, adopted by more than 30 states and the District of Columbia, distribution of the assets can be deferred until the child reaches age 21, or 25 in the case of California. Also, a UTMA account allows you to transfer a wider range of property, including real estate, royalties, patents, and paintings.

STRATEGIC INVESTING

How to invest college savings is another matter. You want your money to earn as much as possible (without taking any serious risks, of course) and be taxed as little as possible. Since you do not need any current income from your college fund, you want your money to grow in tax-deferred growth investments.

Choose your investments to correspond with your child's age. When he or she is under 14, go for growth. Growth stocks and growth mutual funds minimize current income and give you a good shot at keeping up with inflation. Hold the stock investments until your child turns 14; when you sell the stocks the capital gains will be taxed at the child's lower rate. Then switch into relatively conservative income producing assets such as certificates of deposit or bonds that will mature as you need them.

Bonds

Zero-coupon municipal bonds are particularly well suited to saving for college. The bond does not pay semiannual interest; you buy it at a deep discount off the face value and get the full amount when it comes due. One technique often used with zeros or stripped municipal bonds (essentially the same as zeros) is to stagger their maturity dates so that they come due over the four college years. Or you could invest in a unit trust, which pools many different zero-coupon issues.

Series EE Savings Bonds are very safe and can also be purchased so that the time they come due coincides with your child's college years. Interest on bonds purchased after January 1, 1990, for families with incomes under $60,000 is tax-free (tax-reduced for incomes up to $90,000), *if* the bonds are cashed to pay for college expenses. The minimum yield on bonds held for five years is 6 percent. The interest rate will be increased as the average return on five-year Treasury bills increases. The tax-free feature of Savings Bonds should make their actual yield comparable to those of certificates of deposit and money market funds.

Life insurance

Another possible way to save for college is through life insurance. For a minimum of $5,000 you can get a single-premium whole life policy with an 8 percent yield guaranteed for one to five years. The big benefit is that you can let your earnings grow tax-free until your children start college, then borrow the earnings, interest-free, to pay tuition. What's more, most colleges will not consider the value of your policy among your family's assets as they would stocks, mutual funds, or other investments when determining your child's eligibility for college aid.

Annuities

A deferred annuity can also be a useful way to accumulate money for college expenses. An annuity is an agreement between you and an insurance company; you pay one or more payments and the company agrees to pay you a lump sum or periodic payments starting at some future date.

The advantage of an annuity for college funding is that, while your money is invested, it is growing at a tax-deferred rate; you don't pay taxes on any gain until you cash in the annuity or start receiving payments from the contract. The disadvantage is that, under most circumstances, if you cash in the contract before age 59¹/₂, you will have to pay a 10 percent penalty on the *growth* in your investment. Some contracts, however, will permit you to borrow against the annuity; this is to your advantage if you will need the money before you reach age 59¹/₂.

Annuities can be single premium (you pay one lump sum, up front) or annual premium (you make annual payments for a period of time). The contract can be for a fixed annuity which generally offers a guaranteed minimum rate of return, or for a variable annuity. The return on a variable depends on how well the investments in your annuity performed. For purposes of college financial planning, the fixed annuity may be the better choice.

Annuities are most useful when college expenses are at least 8 to 10 years away, allowing adequate time for tax-deferred growth. You should look carefully at the tax consequences before investing in an annuity, but you may well find it a good choice.

Minor's trust

If you are a high-earning couple, another way to pass the bucks to your kids is with a minor's trust, also known as a 2503(c) trust. When substantial amounts of money are at stake—at least $50,000—the expense of setting up such a trust (about $500) is more than offset by its advantages. The first $5,000 earned by the trust, no matter what the child's age, is taxed at 15 percent; any amount above that is taxed at 28 percent. Also, the trustee, normally a parent, controls the income and principal until the child reaches 21, as with a UTMA. But in a minor's trust your child has only 30 to 60 days from the time he or she turns 21 to demand the assets from the trust; if the child fails to do so, the trust continues until the time you have specified in the trust agreement.

Children's earnings

There is one old-fashioned way to provide income to your

children and beat the kiddie tax: make them earn it. Income earned by a child from a job is taxed at the child's rate. It is tax-free up to $3,000, indexed for inflation. If you own your own business and put your kids on the payroll, you can deduct the wages as a business expense. If they are under 18, you do not have to pay Social Security taxes. Of course, the wage has to be commensurate with the job. But even if your youngster is at an age where he or she is more likely to eat stamps than lick them, you can employ your toddler as a model or actor to advertise your business. Do not be too generous with your Shirley Temple, however, or the IRS will have the last licks.

WHEN TIMING COUNTS

If you opt for a custodial account, you should keep your child's age in mind when making gifts. Richard Coppage and Sidney Baxendale, accounting professors at the University of Louisville, have computed the ideal amounts of equal, annual parental gifts in custodial accounts to take maximum advantage of the lower, after 14, tax rate and allow you to still come up with the necessary cash for college. Assuming a yield of 8 percent annually, and a parental marginal tax rate of 28 percent, the professors calculate that parents of a newborn, for example, would pay $11,917 less in taxes by shifting assets to their children.

Current age of child	Annual gift	Number of gifts	Accumulated net amount	Tax savings
Newborn	$ 5,232	19	$ 185,000	$ 11,917
5 year old	5,650	14	124,000	7,252
10 year old	7,427	9	88,500	3,997
15 year old	14,777	4	63,000	1,201

CHAPTER VII

Planning for the future

W hen you are in your late twenties or thirties, caught up in demanding careers and enjoying the two-paycheck life, the last thing on your mind is getting older and all that it implies: planning for your retirement, thinking about who would care for your children if you both died prematurely, and deciding how you want to protect your property for your heirs. But the sooner you start thinking about these matters, the more time you will have to feather your retirement nest and the less you will have to worry about your assets falling into the wrong hands.

RETIREMENT PLANNING

How much you will need to save for your retirement depends on a number of variables that you probably cannot determine right now: inflation, your age when you retire, your life expectancy, the size of your Social Security benefit and company pension plan, and how you plan to spend your retirement. Tanning in Tahiti? Teeing off in Tucson? Tending to the garden in your own backyard? Depending on how much, and how well, you invest on your own, it is unrealistic to count on an annual income equal to your greatest earnings, presumably in your last year before retirement. Chances are you won't need that much income anyway since your expenses in retirement will likely decrease. Your tax bill, for example, will probably go down, as will your housing costs if you are close to paying off your mortgage. So aim for a retirement income that is at least 70 to 80 percent of your gross earnings before retirement.

Where will it come from? Most people put it together from three sources: Social Security, company pensions or Keogh plans, and personal savings and investments.

Don't count on Social Security for much. There's no telling how generous Uncle Sam will be when you retire. Compared with your parents' benefits, though, you will probably have to wait longer to start receiving a Social Security check and that check will represent a lower percentage of your pre-retirement salary. The Social Security Administration will send you a free estimate of your future earnings if you fill out and send in a simple form. To get a copy of this form, call (800) 937-2000 and ask for form SSA-7004, the Request for Earnings and Benefit Estimate Statement.

If you are lucky, your company pensions or Keogh plans will make up the difference. But not many people retire with pension plans that generous. In fact, the Social Security Administration estimates that the average retiree living on over $20,000 a year gets only 42 percent of that income from Social Security and pension plans.

That leaves personal savings and investments. You had better have some. Suppose you decide you want $30,000 a year over and above Social Security and pension income in order to keep yourselves in the style you have grown accustomed to as a two-career couple. You will probably need well over $500,000 to produce that income from fixed assets and at the same time keep some percentage of your portfolio in growth-oriented investments that will help you keep pace with inflation.

YOUR PENSION BENEFITS

How much of a pension benefit you receive when you retire will depend on your salary as well as your years with the company. Loyalty pays off. If you work for the same company for 30 years, your pension could be somewhere from 30 to 70 percent of your last year's salary. But if you bounce from job to job, you may find that you have no vested pension fund at all.

While you wouldn't choose a job because of its pension plan, you should know exactly what your company offers in the way of retirement benefits. Basically, employee benefit plans fall into two major categories: defined benefit and defined contribution. In defined benefit plans, the company determines how much you will get based on your earnings and length of service and then pays the money out, usually monthly, when you retire. You have no control over the amount or the management of it and you must be vested in the plan—after five to seven years of service—in order to be entitled to your pension when you reach retirement age.

Defined contribution plans are matching programs in which a company contributes a certain percentage—usually 50 percent—of what you put in, and profit-sharing plans, where the employer adds a portion of profits to your savings. Some companies also offer employee stock-ownership plans (ESOPs). In these, the employer will match up to 50 percent of the sum you invest in shares of company stock. Vesting in these plans usually occurs in from one to three years, but your own contributions are 100 percent yours to take (and roll over into a tax-deferred Individual Retirement Account—IRA—if you have not reached retirement age) whenever you leave the company.

Many companies allow you to make contributions through payroll deduction programs known as 401(k) plans. This is the optimal way to save for retirement. Your annual contribution is excluded from your taxable income and you may enjoy an immediate gain on your investment because many employers match at least a percentage of your contribution. Also, the earnings are not taxed until you start to withdraw them (no earlier than $59\frac{1}{2}$ or else you pay a penalty). If you switch jobs, you can roll over the fund into an Individual Retirement Account and still get the tax-deferred earnings. See Chapter III for a further discussion of IRAs.

Defined-contribution plans may also give you some choice in your pension investments. The options might include stock in your company, portfolios of stocks and bonds that operate a lot like mutual funds, and guaranteed investment contracts that promise a fixed rate of return. Usually, you are asked to choose how you want your money invested annually. The options you choose should depend on your tolerance for risk as well as how near you are to retirement. The younger you are, the more you should consider going for growth in a stock fund. Even if the market takes a tumble in a given year, you have got years to make up the loss. Historically, stocks have outperformed fixed-rate investments over a period of time.

INVESTING ON YOUR OWN

Ideally, you should aim to save about 10 percent of your pretax income toward retirement, including your contributions to a Keogh or company plan. In choosing investments, your objectives should be long-term growth and tax savings. A well-balanced retirement portfolio at age 35 might include growth stocks or mutual funds that hold such shares (50 percent), real estate and precious metals (15 percent), and short- and long-term fixed income investments such as money market funds, certificates of deposit, bonds, or annuities.

Investing in IRAs, Keoghs, or company savings plans will maximize tax savings. You should also consider cash-value whole life or universal life insurance policies to shelter earnings on investments for retirement. You can borrow against the cash value at any age at reasonable interest rates without worrying about paying a penalty.

When making a choice between investing in a tax-exempt security or a taxable one, do not make the mistake of avoiding taxes just for the sake of avoiding them. What you are interested in is the after-tax return you will get. Suppose you are in a 28 percent federal and 8 percent state tax bracket. Here's how you would analyze a tax-exempt yield of 7¹/₂ percent from a municipal bond issued in your state.

1. Because state taxes are deductible from federal taxes, you must calculate your effective state tax. Simply multiply 8 percent by 72 percent (100 percent minus your federal tax rate of 28 percent).
   That calculation is .08 x .72 = .057

2. Add your effective tax rate to your federal tax rate:
   28% + 5.7% = 33.7%

3. Use the following formula:

$$\frac{7.5\%}{66.3\% \ (100\%-33.7\%)} = 11.3\%$$

If you can get a taxable yield better than 11.3 percent, you are better off than you are with the 7¹/₂ percent tax-free yield. Naturally, you must also consider the risk factor when making such a decision.

Finally, do not invest in a vacuum. Your own investment portfolio should counterbalance both of your company benefits as well as your careers. If you are a salesperson who works on commissions or a freelance artist and your income is erratic, your investments should sit in stodgier vehicles such as stocks that promise growth plus income, CDs, or Treasury bills. If, on the other hand, you both have secure jobs with solid benefits packages, you might want to try to get a bit more bang from your bucks. Once you near retirement age, however, you will want to shift your investment portfolio into income-producing investments such as bond mutual funds, Treasury bills, or money market mutual funds.

WHERE THERE'S A WILL

Unpleasant as the process of estate planning may be, the alternative—doing nothing—is worse. If you and your spouse do not already have wills (two-thirds of all Americans do not) here's what could happen:

1. Your heirs' inheritance will be decided by state laws that do not take into account your wishes about who should get what. In most states, your assets are divided among your spouse and children, often with half to two-thirds going to the children.

2. If both of you should die at the same time, the state will also decide who will be the guardian of your children if they are under 18. If only one of you dies, the surviving spouse would automatically have custody and no special provision in the will is necessary.

3. Even with a will, your heirs may have to pay some estate taxes. But by setting up trusts, a married couple can pass as much as $1.2 million to their heirs without passing on a federal estate tax bill in the bargain.

If you have a carefully executed estate plan, your heirs can minimize any problems with probate, the lengthy legal process in which your assets are valued and your will is proved valid.

To make sure that your wills are drawn up properly, you will need to hire a lawyer who is knowledgeable about estate planning. Perhaps your financial planner or an attorney you use for other matters has a recommendation. You could also call the local bar association for names.

Even if you do not have children, a will is necessary. But if you do it is imperative that you have one drafted. Only in a will can you name the guardians to care for your children and manage their inheritances. Choosing the right person to be the guardian for your children isn't easy. Lawyers advise that you choose siblings instead of your aging parents. But if you are set on your folks because you like the job they did with you, you may want to name one or two successors—just in case. If, however, your relationship with your family is strained, there is no reason why you can't name close friends whose values and lifestyles are similar to your own. Ideally you should choose a couple rather than a single person so that the child will be raised in a household with adults of both sexes. But lawyers advise you to make only one spouse the legal guardian in case they divorce sometime in the future.

Naming a guardian in your will is binding unless the party refuses the responsibility. Ask the person if he or she will undertake the job. Also, double-check with an alternate guardian. If your guardian of choice were to refuse the job after your death, the court would be responsible for finding and appointing a substitute.

Guardians often have a dual role: to handle the child's day-to-day upbringing and to take charge of his or her financial affairs. But parents can appoint different guardians for each set of responsibilities. If your chosen guardian is very loving but not too adept at handling money, this system lets you select someone else to manage your child's inheritance. A guardian of the purse must submit an annual accounting to the court of how he or she is using the funds. The financial guardian must get permission from the court to spend large sums of money—to buy a teenager a car, say. While this may prevent the guardian from misusing the children's inheritances, it also gives a judge who is unfamiliar with your financial goals and investment philosophy power over how your legacy is managed and spent.

The trusts to trust

To spare your children such an eventuality, you should have a trust provision in your will to govern your children's inheritances. With a trust, you need not name a guardian of your children's assets (you still must name a guardian to care for them). The trust document spells out how you want the money in the trust spent and names a trustee—a financially savvy friend, relative, or professional—who is responsible for managing the funds on behalf of the beneficiary, your child or children. Another advantage of a trust is that you can keep your offspring from touching the trust principal until you think they are mature enough to manage the money on their own. When you leave property to your children in your will without a trust provision, they are entitled to claim their inheritances at the age of majority—18 in most states.

In general, a trust is a legal vehicle whereby a grantor—the person who sets up the trust—has property held within the trust for one or more beneficiaries. There are two basic types of trusts, testamentary and living. A testamentary trust is part of your will and takes effect when you die.

A living or inter vivos trust begins while you are still living. In a revocable living trust, you continue to control the trust property: you can change the trust's provisions, terminate it, and, in some cases, even serve as trustee. Assets in a revocable trust are part of your taxable estate. However, property in such a trust also bypasses probate. If you establish an irrevocable living trust, you cannot control the assets in it or change its provisions. The advantage of such a trust is that the property in it is not included in your estate for the purpose of calculating estate taxes. A testamentary trust for your minor children that becomes irrevocable upon your death is included in your taxable estate because you controlled the property in it during your lifetime.

With astute planning, most estates can avoid federal and state taxation. You are allowed to make gifts of any size and leave an estate of any value to your spouse tax-free. The problem comes when your spouse dies and the property passes to your heirs. A bypass testamentary trust lets a married couple pass as much as $1.2 million to their heirs tax-free. Let's say a husband has accumulated $1.2 million in assets. In his will he leaves half the property, $600,000, to a bypass trust, the income from which goes to his wife for her lifetime. Their children become the beneficiaries of the trust after she dies. The husband's estate owes no tax because he is allowed to leave up to $600,000 free of federal estate or gift tax. Because the wife does not control the property in the trust, it is excluded from her estate, too. The husband leaves the remaining $600,000 to his spouse and she pays no taxes because of the marital deduction. She can then use her $600,000 exemption to leave it to the children tax-free.

If your spouse is not in a position to manage your assets you can leave those assets in a trust in which the contents are not subject to estate tax. There are two types of marital deduction trusts, and in both the spouse receives all the income the trust produces. With a general power of appointment trust, your spouse determines who gets the assets from the trust after he or she dies. With a qualified terminable interest property (Q-TIP) trust, you choose the eventual heirs.

When you are attending to these matters, you should name a contingent beneficiary on your life insurance policy, your retirement account, lump-sum disability protection plan, and company retirement plan. A surviving spouse is usually the principal beneficiary for these accounts. You need to choose a contingent beneficiary—generally your child—in case both of you die at the same time.

OPTIONS FOR OWNERSHIP

For many affluent two-income couples, owning property jointly can be a costly mistake since it inadvertently guarantees that if one spouse dies, all their property will be lumped together in his or her estate. The maximum that can be passed on to your heirs tax-free is $600,000. But consider that as a two-income couple, your assets may well appreciate beyond that amount and would be subject to estate taxes of between 37 to 55 percent of anything above $600,000. There are other ways to own property that can shelter as much as $1.2 million from federal inheritance taxes. Here are four alternatives:

Joint tenancy with the right of survivorship

When a couple owns property in this way, each of them is a "joint tenant" with an equal share of the property. Theoretically you can sell or give away your interest without getting the consent of your mate. Because of this "severability," however, a creditor can seize a debtor's share of the property and perhaps force the other owner to sell. When you die, your share does not go into your estate; ownership automatically passes to the surviving tenant, in this case your spouse. Estate planners caution that a survivorship interest can be complicated by greedy beneficiaries or inconsistent provisions in a will. So your wishes as set forth in your will should be crystal clear.

Tenancy by the entirety

Only married couples can qualify for this type of ownership. You and your spouse are equal owners of the property and when one of you dies, the interest is automatically transferred to your mate. The advantage over joint tenancy is that one spouse cannot sell or give away his or her interest. This gives the couple more protection against creditors.

Tenancy in common

Those who hold property as tenants in common can own equal or unequal shares. They can sell their interest without getting permission from the other tenant and leave their shares to whomever they please. This approach is probably best for unmarried couples living together.

Community property

If you live in one of the nine states (Arizona, California, Idaho, Louisiana, Nevada, New Mexico, Texas, Washington, and Wisconsin) with community property laws, any income you earn during your marriage and all the assets you acquire are equally owned. The only exceptions are individual gifts received and inheritances. When the first spouse dies, half of his or her share of community property passes to the surviving spouse; the other half goes to the beneficiary named in the will of the spouse who died.

CHAPTER VIII

All in the family

For many two-career couples finding the time to spend relaxing together or enjoying family life has taken on just as much if not more urgency than making money. In fact, a considerable chunk of our expendable income goes toward freeing up more of our time: gourmet take-out dinners, car phones, answering machines to screen out unwanted calls, and shopping by catalog or computer. Witness also the growing number of service businesses that will do anything to help you lighten your load, from renewing your driver's license to organizing your closet to organizing your life. Of course it is work that takes up most of our waking hours. But there are ways to cut back.

CAREER COMPROMISES

When it is just the two of you, two careers are demanding but manageable. As an ambitious couple you are soulmates as well as playmates, and without having to wake up for 2 a.m. feedings, you have got energy to spare. But when baby makes three, your world turns upside down. You are constantly feeling torn between your professional life and your life as a parent and you are sure you are failing at both.

Sometimes the pressures are so great that one parent—more often the mother—feels that she must pocket her professional aspirations. But that could be a big mistake. Not only do you have to manage on one income, but the frustration and bitterness over giving up a promising professional life could take an even greater toll on family life. Staying at home and bringing up your children full-time is fine, if that's your choice after considering the alternatives. But if a mother is going to feel unfulfilled at home, the whole family probably is better off if she goes back to the job.

Fortunately, there are other options to consider short of dropping out. Consider taking a longer maternity leave—at least four months. This will give you the needed time to be with and get to know your baby. If you are as indispensable as your boss claims you are, ask him or her to extend your unpaid maternity (or paternity) leave to, say, six months. Some companies are taking the lead on this issue. At Merck, the pharmaceutical company, for example, new mothers can go on unpaid leave for up to 18 months after their child is born.

Rather than give up your career altogether, consider switching to a more accommodating line of work or a more accommodating employer. Your options will depend on the stability and size of your spouse's income and your flexibility. The careers that are most compatible with raising children are those where you can call your own shots: real estate, freelance writing, word processing and typing, commission sales, and independent legal work, for example.

HOME SWEET HOME

If you have an entrepreneurial bent, working at home, or starting a business from home, has its advantages as well as its drawbacks. All you need is a personal computer, a facsimile (FAX) machine, and discount long-distance telephone service. Consider also that a home business can be a terrific tax shelter, letting you write off, among other things, portions of your rent or mortgage. But the biggest boon to working parents is the flexibility to quit work early to attend that Little League game or take a day off to accompany your child on a class trip.

Real life, real answers.

When Barbara Kaplan's son Marcus was 18 months old, she decided that she was missing out. Marcus was with his full-time babysitter when he said his first word and when he took his first step. Barbara didn't want another milestone to pass without her having at least a better shot at being around. The Kaplans decided they could give up some of their joint $64,000 income (she earned $30,000 as an account executive for a public relations firm and her husband, David, was a $34,000-a-year electrical engineer) so that Barbara could spend more time with their son.

The following fall Barbara dismissed her nanny and enrolled Marcus in a half-day toddler's program, trimming her monthly child-care costs from $800 a month plus taxes to $350 a month, and freeing herself up for full mornings to pursue a freelance public relations consulting business. She landed one account—an auto service franchise organization—right away; it paid her $1,000 a month. When she added her child-care savings ($450 plus a month), her savings on clothes and dry cleaning ($60), lunches out ($60), and transportation ($50), Barbara realized that if she had one other account bringing in $880 she would equal her previous full-time income. That was before she even considered the tax benefits of operating a business at home: mortgage, utilities, computer, and telephone deductions, adding up to about $400 a month in write-offs. Clearly Barbara's decision was going to pay off in more ways than one.

On the other hand, if you are used to working in an office, you might miss the stimulation of a corporate environment or the camaraderie of your peers. And if your child is not yet in school, you will still have to solve the babysitting dilemma. It is tough to write a convincing brief with a baby wailing in the next room.

Perhaps you are thinking about joining the ranks of other moms and pops who are starting mom-and-pop businesses. Unless the two of you have worked together before, you will have to make sure that you are professionally as well as personally compatible. The prerequisites for a successful business relationship are similar to those for a happy marriage: a strong desire to be together, agreement on your basic goals, openness to each other's ideas, and objectivity in dealing with problems. You should be clear about each partner's responsibilities. Depending on the type of business you pursue, and whether or not it is home-based, you have to be prepared with enough capital not only to start the business but to cover your living expenses until the business shows a profit. You might also have to prepare yourselves to work long and hard hours, a feat not necessarily compatible with child-raising.

If you are not about to switch careers or follow a home-bound career path, consider changing to a more understanding employer in your field whose benefits, programs, and attitudes reflect a sensitivity to the conflicts between job and family. Most of IBM's 240,000 employees nationwide, for example, choose their own hours. Some can work out their own schedules with their supervisors while others can begin or end their workdays earlier or later than other colleagues.

If you are reluctant to change careers or companies, per-haps you can scale back the number of hours you work. Of course, you will pay dearly in pennies and promotions for being on the "Mommy Track." But for many women, the detour is worth it. Janet Shane, 35, a commercial artist in Minneapolis, was able to talk the head of her advertising firm into a part-time job for two years. As long as she meets her deadlines, she can do some of her work at home.

BEING TOGETHER

When working parents try too hard to create that "quality time" together, quality time becomes more of a pressure than a joy. Parents should try to get close to their children from the moment they walk in the door so that everything that follows becomes family time: playing, talking, eating, and working. Parents can involve their children in their chores whether it's tossing a salad or taking out the garbage. If you bring paperwork home, you can do your homework together with your kids. You are right there if they have questions and the sense of togetherness will be reassuring to all of you. Children who participate in the family's solutions will be better able to handle the stresses in their own lives as they grow up.

CHILDREN AND MONEY

If you familiarize your children with family finances when they are young, chances are they will be better prepared to deal with money in a responsible way when they grow up. Being open and informative with children also makes them more secure and gives them more reasonable expectations. However, you should make sure that what you tell children is appropriate for their age.

Children under 10, for example, should know what you need money for, how people earn money in general, and how you earn it in particular. Without pounding away at how hard you both work, show your children by taking them to the office with you one day, if possible, and letting them see what you do. Telling your children the dollar amount you earn is unnecessary. But if a child asks how much money you make, you could, for example, answer that your family earns enough so that you can live in a comfortable house, afford annual vacations, and send the children to college. As the child grows older and more discreet, you may want to be more specific about your earnings.

When a child is old enough to earn an allowance, say age eight, he or she is old enough to get some basic lessons in budgeting. The child should learn, for example, to live within his or her means. As your children mature you can teach them about saving up for things they cannot afford and helping those who are less fortunate. The amount of allowance should grow according to your child's needs: bus fare, lunch money, snacks, movies, clothes, and savings.

Parents should solicit the opinions of their children on money-related matters that affect the whole family. If you and your spouse wonder whether to skip the presents and take the family skiing in Utah next Christmas, consider your kids' opinions too. If you are facing some financial difficulties, it is best to tell your offspring the truth since they are bound to know something is amiss anyway. What they imagine is wrong may be worse than the reality.

TAKE THEM ALONG

Vacations are an important way for the two-career family to unwind together. For some parents the thought of a family vacation conjures up images of hot tempers, cold stares, cramped quarters, and little loose change. But traveling with your tots or teens in tow need not be a disaster. For one thing, more and more resorts, airlines, and cruise ships are courting families with a slew of services and incentives. If you and your children plan your vacation with everyone's needs in mind, you will find more rewards than rigors.

Work out as many of the details of the trip ahead of time as possible. Will you have to pack your Pampers or can you buy them at your destination? Have you reserved a crib and/or high chair in advance? Do you know whether you will be able to warm the baby's bottle on the plane? Set some ground rules too. To avoid tantrums at stores or souvenir counters, give each child an allowance for such treasures at the beginning of each trip. Be flexible and do not overschedule. This is your time to relax together, so do not pack your day so full that you have no time to kick your feet in a water fountain or romp in a local park.

CHAPTER IX

Yours, mine, and ours: commingled families

Even more than other working couples with kids, reconstituted families find that life is hectic and time with their children comes at a premium. They also worry about paying the piles of bills, being able to finance college, and preparing for retirement. But unlike other families, commingled couples must cope with particularly delicate, emotionally charged financial issues such as who pays for what, who leaves how much to which child, and what would happen if one of us dies while the children are still young? Careful planning, keeping the lines of communication open, and keeping a sense of humor can help resolve some problems.

Ideally, couples with kids who are about to marry again ought to settle most of their money matters ahead of time. Deciding where you will live is one of the first orders of business. If you can start fresh in a new home, you will be better off. If you opt for one of your old homesteads, you may be plagued by unpleasant memories and uneasy children. Both married for the second time, Stan and Roz Cohen of Westchester, New York, moved into the house where Roz had lived in her first marriage. They regret that they didn't start off on neutral territory. "Stan's children felt like trespassers and mine did little to make them feel otherwise," says Roz.

Buying a house or a condo together does not mean that each spouse has to split the down payment exactly in half or go

50/50 on the monthly mortgage bill. But if each of you has a stake in your home, it will be more "ours" than "yours" or "mine." Before you buy your home, think about how you want to take title to the property; you will probably want to leave some or all of your share to your children (see Chapter VII). Usually couples buy a home as joint tenants with a right of survivorship. That means that when one dies, the other automatically becomes the sole owner. Parents of commingled families are better advised to take title as tenants in common. Then, by specifying your wishes in your will, you each can leave your part to whomever you choose.

Many financial advisers encourage blended families to enumerate each person's financial responsibilities in a formal, legally binding prenuptial agreement. Among the most important issues to resolve are how to divvy up child-care costs—from preschool payments to weekly allowances to college funds; whether or not to put all your assets and liabilities in one basket; and what to do when it comes to passing on your accumulated wealth.

No matter what arrangements you choose, you are likely to face some complicated consequences. If you divide the financial responsibility along blood lines, you will have to keep separate budgets for everything. That is not necessarily the best way to foster family togetherness. If you opt to keep your assets separate, the practical choice considering that the divorce rate for second marriages is higher than for first-timers, you may need to do battle with the community property laws in your state. You could execute a "property-status agreement," which specifies who owns what. The parties forfeit any spousal claims to specified assets. This could be done as part of prenuptial agreement or after you are married.

A BLENDED AGENDA

Perhaps the best solution is a compromise. One of the best approaches is to create an overall agenda for the new family and to work out some division of responsibilities. For example, a couple may have three bank accounts—his, hers, and theirs. That gives both spouses a sense of independence and autonomy while sharing family expenses. The common pot might go for food, utilities, housing, household maintenance, joint savings, recreation and entertainment, insurance, and major purchases. Individually, the partners would meet their own obligations: alimony and child support, clothing, medical bills, allowances for their children, or whatever they would define as purely personal expenses.

But such togetherness may not extend to your investment temperaments. If his investment approach is more appropriate to Las Vegas than Wall Street and you favor stodgy municipal bonds and CDs, you may both have to move to the middle when it comes to joint investing. Even if you are compatible in your investment outlook, chances are that your portfolios will need some tinkering to make sure you are properly diversified.

CHECKING YOUR COVERAGE

Your insurance will need a careful going over to make sure that all the members of your blended family are properly covered. Check your health plans to see if you have overlapping coverage that might save you out-of-pocket costs. If you are eliminating one auto policy in favor of another, make sure any teenage speed demons in your new mix are included in the policy. The assets each of you have accumulated may not be enough to provide for both your partner and your children if you die. For that reason many couples starting second marriages increase their life insurance coverage. The amount of insurance can be reduced as children approach adulthood and your need for coverage diminishes.

YOURS, MINE, AND COLLEGE

One of the most difficult aspects of blended family life is the sheer cost of caring for a passel of progeny. With older children from former unions and perhaps younger ones from the remarriage, parents of blended families often find themselves facing child-care expenses over a much longer period than other households. That makes it that much harder to put money away for those all-important financial goals of college tuition and retirement. Just as with any family in need of a budget rehaul (see Chapter II), you must examine your expenses versus your income and see where you can cut back. Mom's haircuts and hand-me-downs from an older stepsister may not go over that well with your 10-year-old-daughter, but a number of small sacrifices can add up to significant savings.

Of course, even with considerable cutbacks, your family may not be able to meet all its financial goals. If you have to choose between accumulating for college and your retirement, cut back on college savings. There are more alternatives to paying for college than there will be when you reach your retirement age. Consider less expensive community colleges or state schools rather than private institutions. Scholarships, grants, student loans, and work-study programs are other options for helping to pay for college.

If you have some money to invest, use investments that are geared to help parents pay for their children's college educations, such as Series EE U.S. Savings Bonds. Interest earned on bonds purchased in 1990 will be exempt from federal taxes if the proceeds are used toward college costs for the purchaser of the bond or his or her immediate family. But nothing's perfect. Once a family's adjusted gross income exceeds $60,000, the exemption begins to phase out. You lose it at $90,000.

PROTECTING YOUR LEGACY

Perhaps the touchiest problem for parents of commingled families is how to divvy up their assets should one of them die. On the one hand, parents want their biological offspring to be protected; yet they do not want to neglect or offend their stepchildren or their spouse.

An economical way for most stepparents to make sure their heirs get what is rightfully theirs is to write a trust provision into their wills. That stipulation is called a testamentary trust (see Chapter VII). You can designate the assets you want to leave to your children and decide how and when they will get them. You could, for example, set it up so that when you die your children will get specific sums through their college years and then get the balance at, say, age 30, when you think they will be mature enough to handle a large amount. If you want your spouse to enjoy the benefits of your wealth while he or she is still living, you can set up a bypass trust. After you die, your spouse would receive any income earned by your assets and, with the trustee's approval, withdraw some of the principal if he or she needs it to pay such expenses as college tuition or medical bills. At the death of your spouse, the assets pass directly to your children.

Any parent with children must have a will that names a guardian for his or her children. But even if your natural son and his stepfather—your husband—are very close, his biological father could win custody if you were to die prematurely.

Afterword

As a two-career family, chances are you already have some of the elements of a sound financial plan already in place. Armed with the information in this book, you should now be ready to fill in the gaps.

Remember, though, that a financial foundation, like Rome, wasn't built in a day. Take your time, sort out your priorities, and take the steps necessary to protect your family's "empire."

Real life, real answers.

The up-to-date library of personal financial information

How to make basic investment decisions
by Neal Ochsner

Planning for a financially secure retirement
by Jim Jenks and Brian Zevnik

How to borrow money and use credit
by Martin Weiss

How to pay for your child's college education
by Chuck Lawliss and Barry McCarty

Your will and estate planning
by Fred Tillman and Susan G. Parker

How to protect your family with insurance
by Virginia Applegarth

The easy family budget
by Jerald W. Mason

How to buy your first home
by Peter Jones

Planning for long-term health care
by Harold Evensky

Financial planning for the two-career family
by Candace E. Trunzo